Who's Afraid of Romanée-Conti?
A Shortcut to Drinking Great Wines

By Dan Keeling

All photography by Benjamin McMahon
apart from:

Tom Cockram, pages 28-29, 65, 249
and 253; Juan Trujillo Andrades
pages 38, 220 and 278; Dan Keeling,
pages 93 and 210; Franck Ribière and
Vérane Frédiani, pages 108, 109, 110
and 112; Courtesy of Martino Manetti,
page 141; Gravner Archive - photo
Maurizio Frullani, page 219; Gail
Skoff, page 222.

Intro Photos

In order of appearance:
Jean-Marc Roulot, Meursault;
Talloulah Dubourg and Hugo Mathurin,
Domaine de Cassiopée, Sampigny-lès-
Maranges; Eleni Vocoret, E&E Vocoret,
Chablis; Marion Nauleau-Mugneret,
Domaine Georges Mugneret-Gibourg,
Vosne-Romanée; François Rousset-
Martin, Nevy-sur-Seille; Tom Myers,
Cantina D'Arcy, Langhe; Hôtel-Dieu
de Beaune; Catharina Sadde, Les
Horées, Beaune; Eduardo Ojeda,
Valdespino, Jerez de la Frontera;
Pierguido Busso, Barbaresco;
Stéphane Tissot, Arbois.

Outro Photos

In order of appearance:
Château Canon's well-stocked
cellar, St-Émilion, Bordeaux;
Frédéric Mugnier, Chambolle-Musigny;
Thierry Allemand, Cornas; next
generation E&E Vocoret, Chablis; Théo
Dancer, Chassagne-Montrachet; Jessica
Litaud, Vergisson; Priorat cellar;
El Celler de Can Roca's wall of Vin
Jaune, Girona; Paola Medina, Bodegas
Williams & Humbert, Jerez de la
Frontera; Marie-Thérèse Chappaz,
Fully, Switzerland.

CONTENTS

FOREWORD

"The unspeakable in pursuit of the uneatable", Oscar Wilde said of the English aristocracy foxhunting. Had he encountered early 21st-century wine writing, he would have witnessed the unreadable in praise of the undrinkable. Puff pieces with a passive respect for hierarchy abound; the contemporary wine press at large on the downhill slide to oblivion.

The profession badly needs disruptors — and in Dan Keeling, we have one. When *Noble Rot*, the magazine he founded with his friend Mark Andrew, burst onto the scene in early 2013, it offered something completely different. Uniting a motley crew of industry pioneers and passionate outsiders (of which I was one), Dan and his contributors took the whole world of wine, from newly fashionable natural vino to the noblest of châteaux, as their domain. From the beginning, they struck just the right balance: irreverent but rigorous, and never afraid to pose uncomfortable questions. They took wine deadly seriously, but not themselves. Perhaps because Dan was new to the game he published brilliantly bold, unorthodox work and *Noble Rot* became not just a cult hit but one of the bastions of contemporary wine culture.

A decade later and *Who's Afraid of Romanée-Conti?* underlines how far Dan has come — even if he still writes with the enthusiasm of a newcomer. Ranging from the limpid mountain whites of the Savoie to the smoking summit reds of Mount Etna and the many different faces of new school Burgundy, the wines championed here are eclectic. Nor will you find any dogma about chaptalisation or sulphites, for Dan is pragmatic in his pursuit of the world's most characterful wines, recognising that there's no one recipe for translating wine's holy trinity of time, place and people.

This book isn't just a compilation of articles (many of which have been updated after original publication in *Noble Rot* and the *FT Weekend Magazine*) with added profiles and recommendations. It's a fully-fledged philosophy of wine. And what's more, it's a philosophy of pleasure, a summary of which wouldn't be a mission statement but something infinitely more usable: a wine list.

Two decades after Jonathan Nossiter's film *Mondovino* (2004), Dan's book also underlines how much the world of wine itself has changed. At the turn of the millennium, we feared globalisation would mean homogenisation, effacing regional traditions, marginalising indigenous grape varieties and imposing a banal 'international style'. That hasn't come to pass. The globalised information economy has in fact cultivated more markets for the most niche and idiosyncratic wines. Today, it's the small, artisanal producers who are thriving; all the while, demographic-driven changes in consumption are eroding the market share of soulless industrial plonk. Regions that had strayed far from their roots are returning to them. *Who's Afraid of Romanée-Conti?* not only offers eloquent testimony to this cultural shift; the writing it contains has also helped to shape it. In many ways, it represents the victory of the outsiders.

William Kelley
Beaune, France

INTRODUCTION

A thirst for thrills

There's a pernicious myth that you need to know much more than you do to enjoy great wine. Ditto that you're either born with a good sense of taste, or you're not; and that identifying a list of fruit aromas in a glass of wine makes it a more meaningful experience. None of this is true. Experts do not feel Chablis more intensely. Explaining when 1962 Mouton Rothschild was harvested, or whether or not it smells of cassis, mint and eucalyptus, isn't a requisite for pleasure. Indeed, wine appreciation's incessant reaching for objective facts about something so intrinsically unknowable often only breaks the spell. No wonder so many intelligent drinkers feel so daunted that they can't keep a single useful bit of knowledge about it in their head.

Don't get me wrong: pulling the legs off vino can be as academically fulfilling as studying quantum physics. But *Who's Afraid of Romanée-Conti?* is more about how drinking great wine makes you feel and celebrating its surrounding culture than what it tastes like, or technical winemaking jargon. Great wine is something to be experienced, whether through visiting new places, meeting new people, discovering gastronomic synergies, or savouring the rush of euphoria as the first sip of alcohol courses through your veins. I hope it passes the acid test for a book of its kind: to inspire, inform and entertain, but above all to make you thirsty for thrilling bottles. There's a universe of wine out there that most of us have never tasted, and now is the time to do it.

I'm a wine snob, I'll be honest with you. Not in terms of treating wine as a status symbol — I'm all for making the good stuff accessible to as many people as possible. But I'm snobbish in the sense of championing 'living wines' over the billions of industrially manufactured dead ones out there. Living wines are, for the most part, made in small quantities by obsessive dreamers, and they feel like they come from a different planet. Like human beings, they are capable of providing exhilarating highs – but also of off days, weeks, or occasionally even years. Some start clumsily and blossom decades later. Others burn brightly then quickly fade away. That living wines reflect the mysterious nature of our own existence is part of why I love them so much.

Anyone who's kicked the barren soil of a chemically treated vineyard compared with a thriving natural one knows that not all grapes are created equal. Sure, "great wine is made in the vineyard" is a galumphing cliché, but having walked in many of the world's top crus and witnessed the tireless work of these dreamers, I'll go all in. Perhaps "great wine is born in the vineyard and lovingly guided with as few compromises as possible" is more accurate. Living wines are full of vitality because they've not been aggressively processed and have been allowed to become what they are. Industrial wines are a series of compromises prioritising profits, as sterile as a pint of UHT milk.

The past couple of decades have been the best period in history to be a wino. When I began to get really interested while still working as a record company A&R man in 2006, Crus Classés Bordeaux were what folks who were 'serious' about wine drank. Yet by 2013, when my passion had deepened – and, wondering what a career change involving wine and food might look like, published the first issue of *Noble Rot* with my friend Mark Andrew – everything the baby boomers thought they knew was being challenged by a younger generation. Since then, the magazine has opened domaine doors that might otherwise have remained closed, helped build Keeling Andrew – our import company representing the world's most exciting *vignerons* – and spawned several Shrine to the Vine shops and Noble Rot restaurants that have won a World Restaurant Award and scooped 'Wine List of the Year' at the National Restaurant Awards an unprecedented five times.

Perhaps the question I get asked the most about this new career in wine is whether I miss working in music. But because the two have a lot in common I haven't missed it for a minute. Just as drinking a great bottle, like hearing a great song, can start a movie playing in your head, so using similar strategies to those I used to find artists to sign for Parlophone Records to find *vignerons* to work with makes me feel like I never left music at all. In both sensory-based métiers I've seen that paying attention is not just, as French philosopher Simone Weil said, "the rarest and purest form of generosity", but the essential ingredient for making creativity worthwhile. Because whether it's Radiohead or Romanée-Conti, the world's most fabled Pinot Noir, there's no point in quality unless you are prepared to listen.

Distinctive wines that have something unique to say are the beating heart of *Who's Afraid of Romanée-Conti?* It begins with the Riesling that sparked my obsession and moves through the holy grail of finding good cheap house wine as a restaurateur to what to pour pals who couldn't care less, when to open young and old bottles, and what it's like to actually drink aforementioned Romanée-Conti, the pinnacle of what wine can achieve. And then how to find alternatives to provide amazing feelings for far less money. In famous European regions we meet winemakers challenging the status quo and redefining what is possible in historically poorly regarded vineyards; take pleasure in off-trend places and styles such as Condrieu, Priorat and rosé Champagne; and discover the lesser-known wines of Switzerland, Corsica and, of course, England. In Jerez, we step into ancient bodegas as priceless as Goya paintings, and taste 300-year-old nectar. While back in Burgundy and Jura we visit subterranean mould-covered cellars that are as much a part of the 'terroir' as the climate, soil and winemaker.

I'm in awe of the uncompromising winemakers featured in this book. Few people know just how much energy and faith they put into their work, the challenges they have overcome to build domaines from scratch, or take care of their family through testing years. The single-minded determination of *vignerons* such as Jean-Marc Roulot, Olivier Collin, Gianfranco Soldera and Jean-Marie Guffens to make their dream wines blows me away, echoing many of the successful artists I met in music. Indeed, it's no exaggeration to say that making wine at this level is art, imbued with its own sense of originality and soul. Over the coming chapters I want to take you on a journey into many of their vineyards and cellars, places normally inaccessible to most people, and inspire you to seek out the treasures within.

Who's Afraid of Romanée-Conti? is a shortcut to drinking great wines, from humble Picpoul de Pinet to the Grands Crus of Burgundy. But if I've learnt anything over the past 15 years, it's that the more you delve into the mysterious puzzle of vino, the more you must accept the absence of certainty — just as in our everyday lives. The poet John Keats wrote that "Beauty is truth, truth beauty — that is all / Ye know on earth, and all ye need to know", referring to what he called 'negative capability' — taking pleasure from inspirational experiences without having to find facts to explain them. What do we really need to know to be worthy of enjoying a great wine? I challenge you to embrace the mystery, and open your mind to more confident, adventurous, pleasurable drinking.

Let me light the way....

KEY TO PRICES

$	Under £15
$$	£15–£30
$$$	£30–£100
$$$$	£100–£1,000
$$$$$	Over £1,000

THE PERFECT GATEWAY WINE

Or how I learnt to love vino and replaced the rave

2008 FE Trimbach
'Cuvée Frédéric
Emile' Riesling
and a variety of
other sauces.

Have you ever been the schmuck who mistakenly orders a bottle of sweet-as-marmalade Sauternes in a restaurant at the beginning of a meal? Or 'creates' a dish as heinous as 'chilli pepper soup', the only thing you can 'cook' at home, by adding copious quantities of chopped red chilli and ground black pepper to the Knorr Chicken Noodle variety? Friends, I'm ashamed to admit to such indiscretions. But there came a time when I finally woke up to gastronomic self-improvement and began taking an interest in something other than just the next weekender, or who's head-lining Glastonbury. 'Replacing the rave' happens to almost all of us in one way or another, whether it means spending your mornings fannying around on the golf course, or reimagining yourself as a reiki master. And so it was, in 2007, that my wife and I enrolled at Leiths School of Food and Wine and on Christie's Wine Course in London to begin our re-education.

My cookery skills may once have been as lacking as the family-planning section of a Catholic pharmacy but Leiths gave us quick kitchen confidence, teaching us how to dice an onion while also allowing us to make lifelong friends. Christie's, too, was a fabulous introduction to something that, unbeknown to me then, would become a second métier. Although at the time I had little idea who course tutors Michael Broadbent and Steven Spurrier were, looking back I now feel as privileged as someone who had been taught basic physics by Albert Einstein. These debonair old-timers had an air of conviviality derived from the enjoyment of the finer things in life, and what they didn't know about the great crus of the world you could write on a Château Margaux cork.

Working with us through classic regions, styles and grape varieties over six weekly evening classes, Broadbent and Spurrier often bamboozled the congregation of trainee actuaries and red-trousered Sloanes with inappropriate details ("on the 16 April 2004 hail decimated part of the vineya..." Zzzzz). But they fuelled my burgeoning interest by adding dimensions to famous names through constant tasting, especially with their choice of benchmark Alsace Riesling—the entry *cuvée* from Maison FE Trimbach. I remember the revelation of putting my nose in the glass as if it were yesterday: the pale liquid's familiar odours of petrol and green apple transporting me straight to my motor-mechanic father's restoration workshop as a child, and hot-wiring a connection between the word 'Riesling' and the evocative taste sensation I'd experienced several times before without ever knowing what it was called.

Back in the present, although my taste has evolved, I still think Maison FE Trimbach makes the quintessential dry Alsatian Riesling. Like a childhood crush, I'll always have a soft spot for its canary-yellow label and angular bottle: if I were asked to recommend an inexpensive, widely available white for someone beginning to explore wine, this could be it. But, for a few quid more, the Trimbach wine I really want to drink is 'Cuvée Frédéric Emile', Trimbach's next notch up, which I discovered soon after finishing Christie's, a Riesling that's been the gateway to infatuation for many winos. Of course, the house also produces 'Clos Ste Hune', which some critics cite as the best wine of any kind (Jancis Robinson picked the 1990 as part of her hypothetical 'last supper' in *Noble Rot* magazine), as well as other single-vineyard Rieslings, and the local specialities Pinot Gris and Gewürztraminer. But for me 'Cuvée Frédéric Emile' hits the sweet spot of affordability, ageability and deliciousness. It's the rare mainstream white wine that can appeal as much to a total beginner as the jaded aficionado.

Maison Trimbach is based in a half-timbered building in fairy-tale Ribeauvillé, and is headed by brothers Jean and Pierre, the twelfth generation of Trimbachs to run the domaine since it was founded in 1626. "I like to say that we kept the good things about Germany—the discipline and the sausages," says Jean, whom I imagine terrorising exchange students with a sense of humour even drier than his wines. Indeed, this border region close to the Rhine has a long history of occupation, a blur of French and German culture that, ironically, has long seen locals viewed with suspicion by both sides. Not Germanic enough for the Germans, nor French enough for the French. The stylistic overlap extends to the local cuisine: specialities such as baeckeoffe ('baker's oven') and choucroute garnie (Alsatian sauerkraut), as well as oodles of sausages and cured meats—hearty foundations for long days exploring the surrounding hillsides and mountains that pair brilliantly with the richness and acidity of 'Cuvée Frédéric Emile', even if it is a white wine.

Frédéric Emile was the 'FE' in Maison FE Trimbach, an ancestor who developed the domaine's expertise and reputation. The wine is made from grapes grown on two steep Grand Cru vineyards in Ribeauvillé overlooking the winery—south-facing Geisberg (which has stony clay and sandstone soils) and east-facing Osterberg (stony clay and marl). The different parcels are vinified separately in an array of steel, concrete and wood vessels, then blended together by winemaker Pierre. But, like the wine's lofty sibling 'Clos Ste Hune', the label of 'Cuvée Frédéric Emile' doesn't reference any vineyards, a hangover from the domaine's long frustration with what it perceived as Alsace's lax rules for classifying Grands Crus, something that has now been remedied by the Appellation d'Origine Contrôlée (AOC) setting requirements for alcohol levels, yields, and so on. Besides, a lack of accreditation has not dented demand for such consistently excellent wines.

"Frédéric Emile isn't just one of the most iconic Rieslings in Alsace, it's one of the most iconic white wines in the world," says Jean, next to gigantic 10,000-litre old oak casks in their cellars. "When people talk about it they don't say 'Riesling' any more—they say Frédéric Emile, or Freddie E, or CFE. I've heard so many nicknames for it." Jean's swagger is justified—when winos start giving affectionate acronyms to your work you know you're doing something right. One of the reasons that there's such deep admiration for 'Cuvée Frédéric Emile' is the wine's ability to evolve over many years. And, unlike more 'made' commercial wines—that is to say those that are overly manipulated to correct 'deficiencies', obscuring interesting vintage variations—every year has something unique to say.

Having not drunk 'Cuvée Frédéric Emile' for a couple of years, I opened several mature vintages in the hope they'd live up to my memories. I needn't have worried as a couple well surpassed them—not easy, as I've often found out when trying to replicate the thrill of past bottles. Attractive petrol aromas are a signature scent. The wines were also uncompromisingly dry, even when the smell of ripe fruits suggested some residual sweetness, with a zippy line of acidity balancing their inherent richness. More specifically, the linear 2011 had crystalline clarity and was entering its prime; the 2008 was a bit looser, with a slightly more muddled tropical/vegetative profile; the sublime 2007 was like biting into a crisp red apple, balancing Alsatian roundness in the mouth with stony freshness; and the golden 2000 was a fabulous advert for ageability. Contrasting opulent, late-summer stone fruit with an austere finish, it was remarkably fresh for such a warm year.

But as much as drinking 'Cuvée Frédéric Emile' is a reliably satisfying end in itself, it has also been my gateway to discovery. It energised me to begin looking for connections to other great Rieslings, beginning at top Alsatian domaines (whose wines I found harder to identify as dry or off-dry before opening—a wider source of frustration that some drinkers share), and on to the German masters, the Austrians, the Australians and beyond. It can also save the day when faced with a mediocre restaurant wine list: 'Cuvée Frédéric Emile' is a classic produced in large enough quantities that there's often a stray bottle to be plucked from among the lacklustre commercial brands. Just as I was on Christie's Wine Course with Broadbent and Spurrier—both of whom have long since departed for the great barrel cellar in the sky—I know I'm in the safest of hands. ●

RIESLINGS TO BE CHEERFUL
A SHORTCUT TO OTHER GREAT ALSATIAN, GERMAN AND AUSTRIAN ESTATES

Jintaro Yura
Le Silence et la Résonance
Alsace, France
$$$

If Trimbach and other domaines such as Albert Boxler represent great classically styled Alsatian wine, producers such as Mathieu Deiss and Jintaro Yura are part of a new generation pushing it on. Yura hails from Japan, where he was exposed to wine through his father's restaurants. Starting his career as a sommelier, he enrolled in wine school and travelled around Burgundy and Waipara before settling in Alsace and working for local domaines. In 2020, Domaine Gross's Vincent Gross helped Yura make his first wine from bought-in fruit using native yeasts, élevage in a variety of containers, and some stirring of the lees — something much more usual in Burgundy than Alsace. Jintaro Yura's lithe, energetic 2022 'Le Silence et la Résonance' is texturally more akin to fine Meursault than many burlier regional wines.

Weingut Keller
Kirchspiel Grosses Gewächs
Rheinhessen, Germany
$$$$

Like all profound revelations, I can picture exactly where I was (the kitchen) and with whom (my pal Matthew) when I tasted Keller's super-mineral 2007 Kirchspiel Grosses Gewächs for the first time. Even though we drank it alongside a legendary bottle from another (then) much more famous producer over dinner, the way it combined the weightiness of dry Grand Cru white Burgundy with a searing line of acidity almost made us shout "Hallelujah!" Indeed, the wine-loving Keller family — Klaus-Peter, Julia and their son Felix — look west to the best of Champagne and the Côte d'Or for inspiration for their similarly refined approach to farming and vinifying their great Rheinhessen crus. Powerful, ripe, intense yet elegant Rieslings, Keller GGs are among Germany's best, fermented to dryness so as not to mask their sense of 'somewhereness'. See also: Keller Riesling 'Von der Fels' ('from the rocks'), a more affordable classic sourced from younger vines across several vineyards.

Joh. Jos. Prüm
Wehlener Sonnenuhr Auslese
Mosel Valley, Germany
$$-$$$$

Bernkastel-Wehlen's Joh. Jos. Prüm
doesn't make dry Riesling, only off-
dry and sweet wines of ethereal
lightness and moderate alcohol
that nowhere else on the planet can
replicate. It harvests late for the
ripest grapes possible, retaining
sugar in the wines when temperatures
in the Mosel Valley drop and many
yeasts stop fermenting, while others
are arrested by chilling them in
temperature-controlled steel tanks.
"It's like a puzzle every year, and
impossible to predict which ferments
will stop," says Katharina Prüm.
"Sometimes we have two tanks of what
we think will be a Spätlese, and
one ferments fast and then stops,
so it might be medium-dry, and then
the other stops early and we blend
the two." Other parts of Germany may
get more alcohol, but mature bottles
of Prüm wines like 1983 Wehlener
Sonnenuhr Auslese are incomparable
high-wire acts. Touch a drop of this
to a dead person's lips and their
heart might start beating again.

Prager
Wachstum Bodenstein Riesling Smaragd
Wachau, Austria
$$-$$$$

Toni Bodenstein describes his
winemaking mission at Prager,
an Austrian winery that pioneered dry
styles in the 1950s, as expressing
the terroir characteristics of
several of Wachau's great vineyards,
"from stone to wine". And of all
such sites, the steep, high-altitude
Wachstum Bodenstein produces the most
intense and stony-mineral of them
all. 'Smaragd' is the region's most
powerful classification, comparable to
dry Auslese in Germany, the wine often
having a dense, creamy/oily texture
with a diverse array of nuances.
Prager produces fantastic Rieslings
that, like Freddie Emile, beginners
may find more accessible than high-
tension off-dry German styles.

2

WHAT TO POUR FOR PEOPLE WHO COULDN'T CARE LESS

Not everyone treats get-togethers as part of the obsessive search for vinous nirvana

Voltaire allegedly loved the Volnay of Louis Latour so much that he saved it for himself, serving the Burgundian winemaker's humbler Beaune to friends. Nixon's advisers reportedly coined the phrase "pulling a Nixon" for the oenophile president's predilection for pouring official guests *vin ordinaire* while surreptitiously drinking First Growth claret. Truly, there are few more heinous crimes in winedom than guzzling all the good stuff while inflicting hateful plonk on others. Of course, this doesn't mean that just because you've invited the odd couple you met at your kids' summer concert to supper, it's time to dust off the Yquem '29. But the golden rule of hospitality is to always be generous to guests. You don't need to spend a fortune serving wines that everyone—not just yourself, topping up from a bottle secretly stashed under the kitchen sink—will enjoy.

I've never concealed a winning vintage while serving lesser wine to others. I imagine the loneliness of keeping such a grubby secret taints the fun. That being said, many wine lovers will at one time or other feel the heartbreak of opening a prized bottle for friends who knock it back, jabbering away about interest rates, *Succession* or what part of Puglia they're going to on holiday. It's best to accept that, for the vast majority, wine exists to complement, rather than corner, the conversation. Those who believe that wine always *is* the conversation would do well to recalibrate their antennas. In such environs it's much better to let sleeping Grands Vins lie, to be shared with one or two like-minded friends who understand that the price of admission to something more than a solid house vino is that they pay just the slightest attention to what's in their glass. The following rules will also be useful to those who do not fixate on wine for so many of their waking hours—if any hours at all.

Before considering what your friends will drink, it's essential to plan how much to give them. I contend that it's prudent to plan on your thirstiest brethren dispatching one or two 750ml bottles each over a four-hour meal. Indeed, nothing says 'good times' more than large-format bottles, the anticipation is proportionally magnified as their size grows to double magnum, jeroboam and so on. Magnums usually taste better than standard bottles because of their slower evolution, containing the same amount of oxygen but double the amount of wine. A six-litre imperial of Bollinger Special Cuvée Brut NV poured by friends to celebrate their nuptials was sensationally good. Whatever you do, don't leave procuring the goodies to the last minute, then fumble proceedings by dividing two Poundland Pinot Grigios into 20 thimble-sized pours – true dinner-party hell.

Always bear in mind that guests are as thirsty for compelling human stories as they are for delicious flavours. All of which are almost always missing from commercial brands, which forgo any semblance of individuality in the quest for consistency (unless, of course, you're a ten-year-old boy who considers the 'legend' that the devil haunted the cellar of Casillero del Diablo as gripping as the siege of Troy). For really characterful dinner-party vino, swerve the supermarkets, and engage a passionate independent merchant who has a personal connection to the small-scale *vignerons* and appellations that populate their cellars. An anecdote about the people or place behind a particular wine is a good way to pique drinkers' interest and increase their enjoyment.

As for a great story, one of the best is how Spain has transformed its reputation as a purveyor of turbocharged, oak-flavoured headache juice into the Most Exciting Wine Country on the Planet™ over the past decade. Region upon region of old vineyards of native varieties have been resurrected by a new generation of DIY *vignerons*, from the Canary Islands and Ribeira Sacra, to the Sierra de Gredos mountains west of Madrid. "Spain is like a castle that's been closed for many years – we're opening the doors and windows and the world is discovering what treasures the castle has inside," Daniel Landi of Gredos' Comando G told me in 2018, since when its glorious Garnachas have risen to Spanish royalty, alongside Vega Sicilia et al. A canny strategy for celebrations is serving the cheapest *cuvées* of such top producers (who take just as much pride in making them). 'La Bruja de Rozas' is a taste of the Comando G magic for a fraction of the price of its single-vineyard crus.

Spain's white wine game is hitting new heights in the Canary Islands with Suertes del Marqués' Listán Blancos, a highly appetising type of liquid rock that, if I didn't know better, I would imagine had seeped through volcanic soils over millennia rather than been born of fruit. Located in the Atlantic, west of the Sahara, Tenerife may seem an unlikely place for fine wine production, but its association stretches back centuries, from British and Irish merchants exporting 15 million litres of Malmsey in 1600, to shipping the last drops of dry Vidonia in 1830. Suertes del Marqués resurrected an elegant take on Vidonia in 2011, but its entry-level 'Trenzado' – named after the local technique *cordón trenzado*, whereby vines are tied off the ground in braids so that they look like gigantic spiders' legs reaching along the Orotava Valley – would be a talking point. Likewise, top Burgundy domaines' generic Bourgognes, and Barolo producers' Langhe Nebbiolos, can be fantastic value.

Suertes del Marqués' Jonatan García Lima is taking Tenerife wine to new heights.

Left:
Marco and
Giancarlo
Petterino in
the courtyard
of their home
and winery
in Gattinara,
Alto Piemonte.

Right:
Petterino's
tiny barrel
cellar. The
over 100-year-
old large oak
botti had to be
assembled in situ
in order to fit.

Serving a mature wine can work well as the centrepiece of a meal. Tertiary aromas such as leather, blood and mushrooms from traditional long-aged styles can be surprising for drinkers only used to the bold fruit of young wines, so it's worth managing expectations by explaining what makes them special. Most guests will look to their host for cues about deliciousness. If you have confidence in your wines, they will too. Petterino Gattinara is a great value choice, a perfumed Spanna (a.k.a. Nebbiolo) grown on volcanic soils in a historic appellation once rated as highly as Barolo by septuagenarian brothers who've both never had partners, let alone left their Alto Piemonte town to see the sea. Matured in ancient oak *botti* for three years and only released after a further decade in bottle, it's as old school as they come.

Lastly, although nothing beats the feeling of sharing great wine, if you are going to guzzle it all yourself, have some self-respect and don't keep it secret. In Paris's Astrance a few years ago, I saw an immaculately attired old boy lunching alone, napkin hanging from his neck by a chain, merrily drinking his way through a bottle of Domaine de la Romanée-Conti Richebourg. Life goals, right there. ●

3

THE RESTAURATEUR'S HOLIEST OF GRAILS

How to find great house wines for a song

Noble Rot restaurants' house white, Chin Chin Vinho Verde.

Never mind the Montrachet, the pre-war vintages of Mouton Rothschild or certain colossally priced natural wines. The biggest challenge facing any restaurateur or sommelier aiming to build a world-class wine list is sniffing out great under-the-radar bottles for a song. None more so than the basic white, red and sparkling house *cuvées* they'll stake their reputation on. Sourcing a bottle that's cheap and not so disgusting that it'd be better used removing congealed Béarnaise from the chef's station is the hospitality game's holiest of grails. It's also the perfect antidote for anyone involved in fine wine who finds themselves detached from the realities of a budget — something that, with rampant inflation climbing over recent years, is easier than ever. Make no mistake, finding good, cheap vino is hard.

The quintessential house wine is a bastion of dependability in the Sturm und Drang of restaurant service. The white and sparkling must be crisp, clean and refreshing with texture and persistence; the red full of pure, juicy fruit with supple tannins. Nothing too challenging, too alcoholic or too sweet. It must be characterful and not prone to faults — a simple pleasure. Many top UK restaurants serve house wines in 125ml measures, six glasses from a 750ml bottle, while the potentially wasteful 175ml and unwieldy 250ml 'trucker pour' are more common in pubs. However, wines served from kegs or boxes were already gaining popularity for their ease of use and cost long before the post-lockdown shortages of glass bottles. Likewise, screw caps at low prices have become widespread.

At Noble Rot restaurants our criteria for a still house wine are that it tastes of what it is, is something we'd happily drink with pals and costs as little as possible (so, after adding the industry standard 70% profit margin for this category plus VAT, it ends up as the cheapest wine on our list). Not too much to ask, you might think, until you taste the oceans of hatefulness that dominate the price point. Sure, nearly all of us have caught 'holiday wine-itis' at one time or another. You chance upon a taverna supplied by a semi-professional local who approaches winemaking like their grand-parents (fermentations from wild yeasts, never filtering) and gets incredible results. But this kind of rustic yet flavoursome wine is rare.

The brutal industrial practices that enable most commercial wines to arrive swiftly and consistently in the market don't make such concessions for taste. Wine quality is hugely affected by farming and the size of production. It becomes thinner over certain yields; fine wines usually range from 20hl/ha to 50hl/ha, while many supermarket specials rise to 150hl/ha. The latter grapes are often grown on chemically ravaged, poorly appointed plains, rather than benevolent organic slopes. Acidity, powdered tannins, enzymes and colour are routinely added by commercial producers keen to remedy their crop's deficiencies while turning a tight margin. This, combined with the rise in average growing temperatures over recent years, means more technically sound wine is made today than ever before. The trouble is that so much of it is lifeless, no matter where in the world it comes from.

If typicity and local traditions are all part of what makes wine culture so endlessly fascinating, it's gratifying to see top artisanal producers such as Sandhi, which makes a house Santa Barbara Chardonnay for San Francisco's Zuni Café, collaborating at the lower end of the market. After opening our first restaurant in 2015, we began looking for a partner to make a house white. I contacted Telmo Rodríguez, Spain's greatest large-scale artisanal winemaker, to ask if he'd create something for us at the £1.50-a-bottle ex-cellar price then common for the category. "My god, Dan! I don't know how to do a wine for that!" he replied. Indeed, sometimes it seems only a miracle worker could fashion anything respectable with land, labour, packaging, storage, transport costs — and profit — factored into the price.

Widening our search to Düsseldorf's ProWein trade fair, we met Antonio Monteiro of northern Portugal's Quinta Do Ermizio and began collaborating on a Vinho Verde. Branding it 'Chin Chin' and commissioning *Noble Rot* magazine illustrator Jose Mendez to create the label, we've lost count of the times it's been erroneously name-checked as a natural wine because of its vibrant aesthetics. It became our house white and that of several other restaurants whose lists we manage. During lockdown it became very popular among people looking to recreate the flourishes of restaurant dining at home, taking on a life of its own. But while 'Chin Chin's' packaging breaks down barriers for drinkers beginning to explore wine, it's the crisp, pure flavours and moderate 11.5% alcohol that make it a crowd pleaser. Indeed, good-quality Vinho Verde — made here from Loureiro and Trajadura — is a brilliant everyday drinker that doesn't cost much money. ●

Like Vinho Verde, Picpoul de Pinet is a light, zesty, saline wine that's a canny choice for inexpensive drinking. Picpoul de Pinet AOC is the only Languedoc appellation exclusively dedicated to producing white wine, and Picpoul (a synonym of Piquepoul, which translates as 'lip stinger' due to its invigorating acidity) is the only grape permitted to be grown there. It is marketed under the slogan 'its terroir is the sea' due to the proximity of the cooling breezes of the Mediterranean, and has a particular affinity with oysters — for once a regional wine board ad campaign tells you all you need to know. Hawksmoor, for example, sells Cave de l'Ormarine Picpoul de Pinet (one of the cooperatives that dominates the appellation) - a perfect friendly session wine for its restaurants.

Côtes du Rhône AOC covers a huge area of southern France, but if you're willing to look there are many lovely, inexpensive wines to be found. The Rhône Valley's most basic appellation, Côtes du Rhône AOC, is made as red, white and rosé from an array of grapes, from Grenache and Mourvèdre to Roussanne and Viognier. While most is made in huge quantities by cooperatives, leading Rhône domaines produce particularly distinguished versions aside from their loftier crus (Domaine Corinne, Jean-Paul &

Loïc Jamet's Côtes du Rhône bests many other producers' Côte-Rôtie, while Château-Grillet makes a superb blanc). On a more basic level, Brawn restaurant's Les Vignerons d'Estézargues Rouge and Core's Domaine du Coulet 'Petit Ours' are perfect examples of overdelivering Côtes du Rhône house reds.

Tempranillo is Spain's signature grape, retaining acidity well in hot climates and made in a range of styles. At Noble Rot restaurants we've always poured a fresh, crowd-pleasing version as our house red. For years this was 'Gran Cerdo', a wine from Rioja that doesn't qualify for the Denominación de Origen (DO), but manages to employ biodynamic farming, native yeasts, no filtration and minimal sulphur additions while staying eminently affordable and consistently clean. Unlike traditional Rioja (where Tempranillo is blended with Garnacha, Graciano, Mazuelo and Viura), it forgoes expensive long ageing in American oak, producing a fruitier style. Likewise, its replacement, 'Don Tinto' — like 'Chin Chin', another collaboration we created for our house red — is organic Tempranillo grown around Toledo, south of Madrid, that is partially aged in oak for a bit more texture. Easy drinking with bright aromatics, it shows how versatile this grape is at the cheaper end of the market.

4

YELLOW WINE/ VIN JAUNE

Dusting off the joys of the Jura's "happy mistake"

François Rousset-
Martin with a
bottle of his
grandfather's
1969 Château-
Chalon 'Sous
Roche', Nevy-sur-
Seille, Jura.

I'll always remember the night I discovered yellow wine — it was the only time fermented grape juice has made me laugh out loud involuntarily. I'd never imagined fine wine could be capable of that. Make you stroke your goatee and weep at its timeless perfection, sure. Or gnash your teeth in disappointment. But as wine appreciation and belly laughs aren't natural bedfellows, I was as surprised at my own incongruous guffawing as I was by the curry aftertaste that 1999 Domaine Berthet-Bondet Château-Chalon left in my mouth. It was an insight into great wine that I'd experienced before — how even when you think you know what to expect, it can feint and shimmy in the most unpredictable ways. And if you think you know great wine but haven't drunk the yellow wine of Jura in eastern France, find yourself a bottle and get ready for some lolz.

That's not to say yellow wine, or Vin Jaune as it's known, isn't serious. I'd even go as far as to say that it can be one of the most complex and age-worthy wines on the planet (stash a bottle in a time capsule and your grandchildren's grandchildren could raise a toast to your memory). I've never seen anyone have a lukewarm reaction to drinking Vin Jaune for the first time, its flavours often discombobulating for beginners. For some, fermented yak dung is more enticing. For others, it's the most exciting taste-bud ping-pong imaginable. From fruitcake and fenugreek to caramel, celery, iodine, peat, toast, mango and whisky, its possible flavours go on and on. This wine is different. Imagine getting your holiday snaps back from the developers in pre-digital days and holding the negatives up to the light. Life is inverted: antique waxed wood floors in place of fresh fruit; an avalanche of burnt-sugar umami, but as dry as a Saudi nightclub.

It's possible to enjoy young Vin Jaune but it begins to relax, deepen and get very interesting around the 15-year mark. 'Rancid walnut' is another typical descriptor, although the adjective does a disservice. There's nothing unpleasant about its wonky nuttiness, caused by sotolon, a chemical by-product of biological ageing (i.e. under a veil of yeast, more about which anon), which is also responsible for the aforementioned curry. Paired with judiciously aged local Comté, Vin Jaune is half of arguably the most delicious symbiotic combination known to man. That such a confluence between grape, yeast and dairy and our capacity for ecstasy exists is almost an argument for intelligent design. Perhaps there really is something up there that loves us and wants us to be happy. Or maybe we lucked out.

An hour's drive eastwards from Burgundy in the foothills of the Alps near the Swiss border, Jura is France's smallest classic wine region, responsible for 0.2% of national annual production. Of these roughly 11 million bottles yellow wine accounts for a mere 5% — so you can bet your local Aldi won't be promoting a BOGOF any time soon. Four Jura appellations — Arbois, Côtes du Jura, L'Étoile and Château-Chalon — make Vin Jaune, but only the latter specialises in it to the exclusion of all other styles, producing refined, delicate wines that set the gold — sorry, yellow — standard. Other grapes are grown around Château-Chalon village, notably Chardonnay, but all forsake the appellation and are designated Côtes du Jura AOC, which is also a wider delimited area of less well-appointed land.

Evidence of Château-Chalon's vineyards dates back to the tenth century when they were owned by the nuns of the local abbey, although biologically aged yellow wines weren't produced until the 17th century (when they were called *vins de garde*, or 'wines for keeping'). The name Vin Jaune only came into common parlance at the beginning of the 19th century, when the sisters got wise to a sticky marketing hook. They were certainly canny businesswomen; to join their order prospective novices had to prove they were descended from a noble bloodline within four generations — a divine way to offload a few cases to the prosperous House of Burgundy, to whom many were related.

Another peculiarity of Vin Jaune is that it's only bottled in glass clavelins. If Burgundy's voluptuous-shaped bottles project sensuality, these short, squat, no-nonsense bruisers look like they're ready to kick your front door in. They store 620ml rather than the conventional 750ml of wine and legend has it the reduced capacity accounts for evaporation during the particularly long time it spends in barrel. But considering Spain ruled Franche-Comté during the 17th century and produced similar bottles, I'd wager that the clavelin, and the fact that both Jura and Jerez make wines under veils of *flor*, aren't purely coincidental. Perhaps Jura farmers had to beat a sharp exit during invasions, or to tend their traditionally diverse crops and livestock, leaving barrels untended, and returned to find a tasty surprise. "Vin Jaune is like tarte tatin," says François Rousset-Martin, one of Château-Chalon's new-old-school masters, "a happy mistake."

There's something simple yet mindbogglingly complex about how yellow wine is made. Powerful, high-acid, late-harvested Savagnin is fermented to dryness, then transferred to old 228-litre Burgundy barrels for a minimum of six years and three months, usually longer. Unlike in the production of nearly all other fine wines, where evaporation is constantly replaced with extra wine to prevent exposure to oxygen, the barrel is left untended,

Mould gold: François Rousset-Martin's thriving barrel cellar, Nevy-sur-Seille, Jura.

leaving a pocket of air at the top. Over the following weeks, a *voile* (a veil of yeast cells, a.k.a. *flor* in Sherry) forms a vacuum seal across the surface of the wine, protecting it from excessive oxygen contact that would turn it into vinegar. Peering into a Vin Jaune barrel I could make out its pock-marked, cracked white surface layer of yeast, glimmering like the moon in the torchlight. Another world, no doubt, although below rather than above.

Such an unusual process produces wines with kaleidoscopic flavours, with only the finest, most concentrated Savagnins able to take on subtle complexities of the *flor* influence while retaining their intrinsic vinous characters. Like Sherry, to which it's sometimes compared, Vin Jaune is often said to be defined by winemaking rather than terroir, or a sense of 'somewhereness'. Yet nowhere else makes anything quite like Château-Chalon. Not only are *vignerons* such as François Rousset-Martin and Stéphane Tissot using meticulous farming to define single-vineyard crus – the latter bottling six different yellow wines a year – but also bear in mind that, when wines spend so long in barrel, terroir is as much to do with the influence of the environment in which they age as the soil on which they're grown. As the wise old French *vignerons*' proverb says: "If you build a cellar and mould doesn't grow, build another elsewhere."

Among the countless bacteria, yeasts and fungi thriving in François Rousset-Martin's 300-year-old Nevy-sur-Seille cellar, no such worries exist. The crooked stone floor, at the bottom of a wooden entrance ladder so perilous that it could make the Dawn Wall seem a leisurely descent, is stacked with mould-covered barrels and crates of bottles. Its walls are black from the evaporation of alcohol. Owning vines in Château-Chalon's most-celebrated *climats*, Rousset-Martin believes that this subterranean world of invisible creatures shapes his stellar wines, and he still has the 1990 Château-Chalon made by his father André – a microbiologist who worked at Beaune Hospital, where the family are from – ageing in cask. "When I visit cellars in Burgundy that are too clean I feel that the wines lose emotions," says Rousset-Martin. "When a cellar has lots of different microorganisms there are never any problems."

Although it is traditional to age yellow wines in warm attics, where large daily and seasonal temperature swings expedite evolution, Rousset-Martin's extended eight-plus years of ageing in his cold cellar provides another level of refinement. His 2012 Château-Chalon 'Vigne aux Dames' ('ladies' vine', in reference to the vineyard's forebears) is among the most delicate Vins Jaunes I've drunk, with a subtle *flor* influence. Like a cross between Jura and Grand Cru Burgundy, its salty fenugreek-fruitcake flavours and visceral energy transported me back to the idyllic slopes where it's grown, softly soundtracked by the burble of the river below. Elsewhere, a very fresh 1969 Château-Chalon 'Sous Roche' – made by Rousset-Martin's great-grandfather – surprised me with a bolt of salted dried mango.

The doors and windows of Vin Jaune cellars are often left open to expose the ageing wines to seasonal changes. They are checked twice yearly by independent oenologists for acetic acid (vinegar) and ethyl acetate (which smells like nail-varnish remover), which ruins some barrels. In fact, although Vin Jaune is sold at a premium, considering its low yields, the resources needed for long *élevage*, its outright rarity, and the amount of spoilage, it really is one of the world's best-value fine wines. As a general rule, cold cellars foster fresher wines, and warm attics more power, but there are, as ever, notable exceptions, such as those produced by retired 'Pope of Arbois', Jacques Puffeney, whose rafter-aged wonders lack nothing for finesse. Grown on Lias marl soils similar to Château-Chalon, Puffeney's 1992, 1990 and 1978 Arbois Vins Jaunes are among my all-time favourites, variations around a theme of apples, meat broth, herbs, nuts and curry.

Vin Jaune is produced by most of the Jura's top names — Overnoy, Ganevat, Château d'Arlay et al. — but Château-Chalon's Domaine Macle is regarded as the granddaddy, ageing its wares in cool 17th-century cellars. Most progressively, Stéphane Tissot ages barrels of wine from the same vineyard in attics and cellars, blending the results. His Vins Jaunes illustrate how Jura's ancient Trias marl soils produce more rustic and powerful wines, such as 'Les Bruyères', and the younger Lias marls more refined ones, such as his beautifully detailed 2008 Château-Chalon. For anyone wondering about the differences between 'biological' and 'oxidative' ageing, Tissot's 2005 Vin Jaune 'Les Bruyères' and 2005 Savagnin 'Dévoilé' started out as 12 barrels of the same wine, but the *flor* died off in five. These five, exposed to oxygen, developed nutty caramel 'oxidative' flavours (released as 'Dévoilé'), while the *flor* continued thriving in the remaining seven, eating into the alcohol after they'd gobbled up all the sugar and producing high levels of acetaldehyde, a chemical compound with a spirit-like odour that is present in particularly high levels in biologically aged wines such as Vin Jaune and Fino Sherry.

But enough science. More important to know is when is the appropriate time to drink Vin Jaune, and what foods it complements. In Jura it is usually served at cellar temperature, like a fine red, either as an aperitif, perhaps with walnuts, or at the end of a meal — with Comté, of course. Having tested it with other cheeses — such as Beaufort Chalet d'Alpage, Chällerhocker and Vacherin Fribourgeois — the only one that came close to Comté's rapture was local Mont d'Or. Like Comté it complements many of the wine's umami characteristics, perhaps because it shares a similar terroir of invisible microorganisms. The classic yellow wine cooked dish, though — and perennial Noble Rot Soho menu fixture — is chicken with morels and Vin Jaune sauce, while the wine's savoury brothiness makes it a particularly good companion to Japanese dashi-based dishes, just as it is to tandoori grills, another winsome marriage. One thing's for sure though: yellow wine is an acquired taste that requires context and an open mind. "It's always surprising to taste Vin Jaune," says Alain de Laguiche of the venerable Château d'Arlay. "You learn more about the wine, and yourself." ●

Right:
The irrepressible Stéphane Tissot, Arbois, Jura.

Overleaf:
(Left) Alain de Laguiche of Château d'Arlay looks through the bunghole of a barrel of Vin Jaune at the veil of flor below (right).

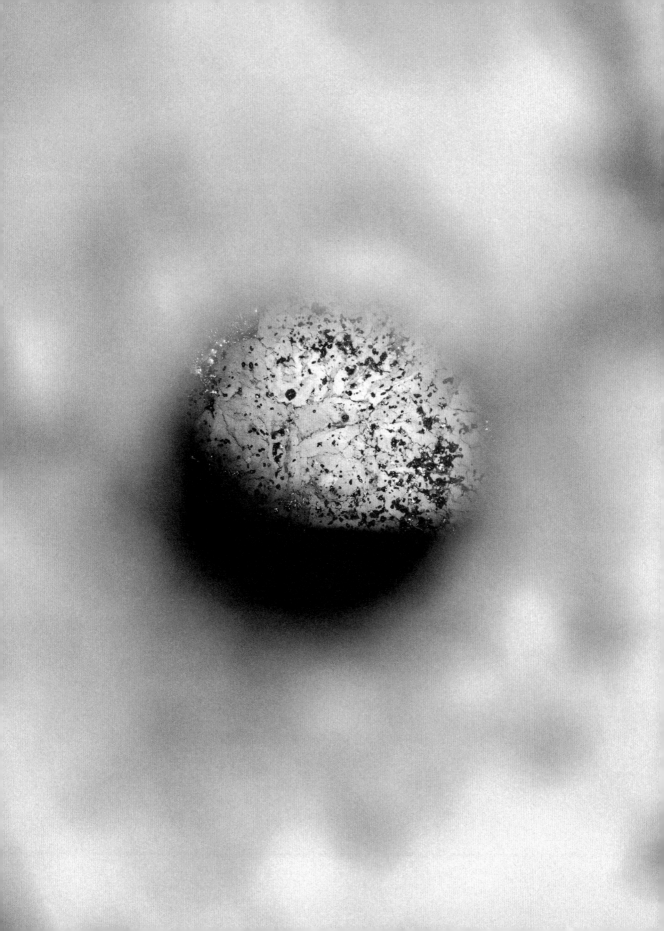

Domaine Tony Bornard
Arbois Pupillin Vin Jaune
$$$

Domaine Labet
Côtes du Jura 'Les Singuliers'
Vin Jaune
$$$

Château d'Arlay
Côtes du Jura Vin Jaune
$$$

Domaine Macle
Château-Chalon
$$$-$$$$

Emmanuel Houillon-Pierre Overnoy
Arbois Pupillin Vin Jaune
$$$$$

Julien Labet makes a vast
array of biologically aged
and 'topped up' wines.

JURA'S 'OUILLÉ' STYLE
AS WELL AS BIOLOGICAL AGEING, VIGNERONS ALSO MAKE CONVENTIONAL WHITES
BY 'TOPPING UP' THEIR BARRELS

François Rousset-Martin
Côtes du Jura 'Sous-Roche' Chardonnay
$$$

A et JF Ganevat
Côtes du Jura 'Les Grands Teppes'
Vieilles Vignes Blanc
$$$

Having grown up in Beaune, François Rousset-Martin understandably also has a passion for making fresh 'ouillé' cuvées where, like the vast majority of wines on the planet, barrels are conventionally 'topped up' to prevent oxygen contact. 'Sous Roche' ('under the rock') is Château-Chalon's pre-eminent vineyard, lying beneath the village's gigantic limestone promontory, but in order to qualify for the appellation its wines are required to be pure Savagnin aged in barrel for a minimum of six years and three months. Rousset-Martin vinifies several other Savagnins and Chardonnays from the cru in a ouillé style, classifying them instead as AOC Côtes du Jura. He's unafraid to sometimes allow a veil to grow for a brief period before beginning topping up, and all his wines speak with a distinct Jura accent, whatever their classification.

Like Rousset-Martin, Jean-François Ganevat trained in Beaune before becoming cellar master at Chassagne-Montrachet's Domaine Jean-Marc Morey. Returning home to Jura having learnt methods such as lees-stirring and rigorously topping up newer oak barrels, he began introducing them to his family domaine — much to the chagrin of his vigneron father. "Up until about 20 years ago, most people in Jura used to leave their wines in barrels without topping up, so they were oxidative to some degree," says Ganevat. He is an influential proponent of biodynamics and low/zero sulphur additions, and his expansive 'Les Grands Teppes Vieilles Vignes', from 100-year-old vines, illustrates Jura's world-class credentials.

5

VALAIS, SWITZERLAND

Alpine wines that tend not to travel

Marie-Thérèse
Chappaz, Valais'
most celebrated
vigneronne,
at home in Fully,
Switzerland.

A word of caution before we begin this chapter about the wines of Valais in the Swiss Alps: they are made in (reassuringly) small quantities and the locals don't care much for sharing. Take 30-something Raphaël Maye of Domaine Simon Maye et Fils in the gorgeous village of Chamoson. He sells most of what he releases each year within a few months, direct from his cellar door. "I don't have to do the extra administration of sending wines to other countries, or wine fairs," says Maye. I say good on him for dodging the mind-numbing tedium of both. And he's not the only one. With a thirsty domestic market and only between 1 and 2% of Swiss production exported, few outsiders ever see — let alone drink — some beautifully crafted wines.

I'm sitting on the terrace of Château de Villa in the heart of the Valais, eyeing a gravestone-sized *carte des vins* while waiters carrying plates of sweet-smelling raclette waft past. A garish plastic affair full of strange names written in a basic sans serif font, the list makes me feel like every drop of vinous knowledge has been sucked from my brain. Swiss vino is almost entirely mysterious to me. But after more than a decade writing about the unknowable puzzle of wine I have learnt to accept that mystery – or the living with the absence of certainty that Keats called 'negative capability' — is part of the deal. So I make like a dead romantic poet and order a Chappaz Fendant 'Coteaux de Plamont' — made by the most celebrated *vigneronne* in the Valais — and marvel at its purity. Besides, it's the only producer name here that I recognise.

I had visited Marie-Thérèse Chappaz (who had sent me to Château de Villa in search of its pre-eminent molten cheese) at her winery in the village of Fully at 2.30pm the previous day. When I arrived, she was in bed. She appeared 20 minutes later wearing her signature round-rimmed spectacles and a stylish safari print dress, explaining that she'd been up in the middle of the night turning on the tap for her vineyard's irrigation system (irrigation is legal in the arid climate of the Valais). Fair enough: turning on a tap located halfway up a mountain accessible only by cable car, where workers who have had an accident can only be rescued by helicopter, in the dark, is not an easy proposition. Besides, who can begrudge a siesta to someone who owns a vineyard called 'The Valley of Hell'?

Combe d'Enfer, to give it its proper name *en français*, is the vinous equivalent of an oyster. Whoever first thought it would be a good idea to grow grapes there — like whoever first thought it a good idea to swallow the contents of a gnarly-looking bivalve — was a visionary with a borderline death wish. Indeed, it's been said that working this gigantic granitic amphitheatre has more in common with rock climbing than farming. Standing at the bottom looking up, I feel as in awe of Chappaz's tireless efforts to repair its terraced stone walls and champion biodynamic treatments here as I am of her wines. She grows 25 different grape varieties to make 26 different *cuvées* (which, like Maye's, are bought almost entirely by the locals), of which I especially adore her whites.

The geographic and cultural similarities between the Valais, in the Upper Rhône Valley, and France's Northern Rhône Valley, relatively nearby to the south-west, are born out in dramatic landscapes and the common success of Syrah and Marsanne grapes. Here, close also to the border with Italy's Valle d'Aosta, the vines grow in poor stony soils at the feet of mountain ranges, where the high costs of working — and the challenges of cheap imports — have shifted growers' aims over the last century from producing large quantities of wine to higher quality. While some Valais wines I taste are as neutral as their motherland was during the war, the cream of the crop can go berry to berry with the best on the planet.

Had I asked the Swiss folks I met to name a great gastronomic wonder of the world, akin, say, to visiting Barolo during truffle season, I'm sure that pairing Fendant with raclette would have topped the list. Never mind Spud-U-Like, Valais is Spud-U-Love country. Everyone, from the hotel receptionist to the taxi driver to Marie-Thérèse Chappaz, adores the national dish of boiled potatoes smothered in melted cheese. Chappaz, for her part, produces four different Fendants (a.k.a. Chasselas in France); serious wines that turn the grape's reputation as a low-rent lubricant for après-ski fondue on its head. In Chappaz's hands, Fendant 'Coteaux de Plamont', from a vineyard at the top of the mountain, is a subtle, rich-fruited white that compensates for its low natural acidity with a fresh, slatey-mineral edge.

If Fendant and raclette are THE match, Chappaz recommends truffle and raclette as the perfect pairing for her Ermitage (just writing these splendid words makes me feel the need to sit down). Ermitage is the Valais name for the white Marsanne grape, christened in honour of sainted Hermitage in France's Northern Rhône Valley, with whose growers they have an agreement to use the name. Mature Chave Hermitage Blanc is one of my death-row wines, and Chappaz's rendition has a similarly gourmand texture. Made from centenarian vines on gneiss, 2021 Grain Ermitage has a delicate, more honeysuckle-dominated fragrance than Hermitage, which

is grown on a mix of soils and also includes Roussanne. The creamy and bitter 2017 Grain Ermitage's fruitcake aromas transported me back to drinking whisky with my grandad. It wasn't quite the big glob of fruit of 2020 Chave Hermitage Blanc — but it is still a wonderfully opulent and indulgent wine.

The indigenous Petite Arvine — a.k.a. 'the pride of the Valais' — makes up the majority of Chappaz's white grapes. Having never encountered it before, my main question is: where the hell has Petite Arvine been all my life? I am not the only outsider to have fallen for this high-acidity, age-worthy, but hard-to-grow white variety that is made in diverse styles, from bone dry to Chappaz's lusciously sweet Grain Noble. Such noted foreign producers as Savoie's Dominique Belluard, Piedmont's Angelo Gaja and Tain l'Hermitage's Michel Chapoutier all liked it so much that they tried planting it in their homelands, with little success. 2018 Chappaz Grain Arvine de Fully is a generous, rounded, citrus-spiked wine infused with the grape's typical salinity. As is Christophe Abbet's 2019 Arvine, a brilliant, distinctive white as pure as Alpine spring water.

Located in a former forge in the village of Martigny, a few minutes' drive from Chappaz, chez Abbet is one of the most atmospheric wineries I've visited. Off to one side of its tasting room, flower petals are strewn over an antique table, while abstract artworks hang from the ceiling — a fitting environment for a *vigneron* with an artistic temperament for whom producing wine is nothing so prosaic as a job. Abbet started out making Gamay in 1985 ("I feel my story in this wine… all wines have stories," he says) and has mastered a range of soulful *cuvées* from native grapes such as Humagne Rouge, Ermitage and a Vin Jaune-esque, biologically aged Marsanne, which he pours for me from custom-made bottles. Aside from his revelatory Petite Arvine, the wonderful smoky-bacon perfume of his 2019 Syrah is a ringer for a top Côte-Rôtie — if Côte-Rôtie was located in the mountains. Which is unsurprising, considering they're grown on similar soils in a continuation of the same valley. You should give it a try — if you can find anyone willing to share. ●

Domaine Marie-Thérèse Chappaz
Grain Ermitage 'Président Troillet'
$$$

Domaine Marie-Thérèse Chappaz
Grain Noble
$$$

Domaine Christophe Abbet
Arvine
$$$

Domaine Christophe Abbet
Syrah
$$$

Domaine Simon Maye et Fils
Syrah 'Vieilles Vignes'
$$$

On yer bike: Raphaël Maye of Domaine
Simon Maye et Fils, Chamoson.

6

A WINE CELLAR STATE OF MIND

Enjoying young or old wines as the mood dictates

Two bottles of 1887 Pol Roger, excavated from a collapsed cellar at the Champagne house's Épernay HQ.

I have an imaginary room beneath my house that's full of rotting fermented grape juice. That this room is, in reality, a darkened corner of a huge bonded storage facility 100 miles west of London is neither here nor there because, as many space-restricted city dwellers know, owning a wine cellar is a state of mind. This state of mind is mostly brimming with happiness, cosseted by the knowledge that regular deposits have been paid into the Bank of Future Vinous Joys. But at other times, it's clouded by mild bewilderment. Because, until the corks are pulled from all those bottles of Meursault, St-Joseph and Brunello di Montalcino slumbering in the faraway gloom, there's absolutely no way of knowing if what's inside them is wonderfully mature or has long since departed. That's the risk you take when you have what our Gallic chums amusedly call '*le goût anglais*', the English taste for old wine.

The term '*le goût anglais*' was originally coined to describe England's historical preference for rich, long-matured styles of Champagne, but our fascination with age extends across the vinous spectrum. American winemaking innovator André Tchelistcheff crudely compared appreciating old wine to relations with a very old lover ("It can be enjoyable. But it requires a bit of imagination"), yet nothing extra is needed to appreciate a time-defying classic such as 1961 Château Latour, a claret so full of vim that it'll surely still be pulling up trees in another 61 years' time.

However, a little imagination is required for 1887 Pol Roger, the most senior champagne I've drunk, rescued from a collapsed cellar at the Grande Marque's Épernay headquarters. While the first bottle was, sadly, dead on arrival, a second's oily texture and faint umami flavours were enriched by knowledge of the 125 years of history that had unfolded around it as it lay undisturbed in northern France.

A T.T.C. Lomelino Verdelho from 1862 long held the record as the oldest wine I'd tasted. This near-indestructible Madeira, a wine produced by alternate cooling and heating, making it among the longest lived of any style, was created from grapes harvested at the time of the American Civil War. But even its 160-year life span seems fleeting when compared with the 1728 Vino Pancho Romano I discovered at Bodegas González Byass in Jerez de Frontera. An inky black nectar that has unbelievably swallowed nearly three centuries and shows no signs of waning, it was a memorably gastronomic experience, rather than merely — as extremely old wines often can be — an intellectual one. Ingesting anything made from fruit ripened by sunbeams that shone on your great-great-great-great-great-great-great-great grandparents is astonishing enough, but this was more vital than many wines a fraction of its age.

"In order to be a great old wine a wine needs to have been a great young one first," González Byass cellar master Antonio Flores told me as I dipped a *venencia* — a pipe-shaped instrument for extracting wine — into the barrel of 1728 Vino Pancho Romano. "Old is only old. How many people do you know who were never happy as a young person and never changed?" This wine, and whoever made it, must have been as Zen as a Buddhist master because the treacly prize that emerged was among the most harmonious things to have ever passed my lips. González Byass bought the single *bota* of 1728 from an *almacenista* in 1841 but never clarified if it was made from stalwart sweet sherry grape Pedro Ximénez or a blend. With 600g of sugar per litre and high acidity, it oscillated back and forth between butterscotch, caramel, salt and citrus like a seismometer gone haywire, before settling on an almost ineffable sensation that I can only describe as celestial walnuts.

Obviously, three centuries is far beyond the limits of most wines' life spans, with the majority designed to be drunk within a couple of years of harvest. But those that have outstanding 'structure' — supernatural levels of sugar and acidity in the case of 1728 Vino Pancho Romano, or a balance of acidity, tannins and other preservative polyphenols with the 1961 Château Latour — allied to dry extract (the material that makes up the body of the wine) far surpass the norm. As time goes by, a wine's edges soften, its fragrance evolves and fruit is subsumed by tertiary aromas such as leather, truffle, blood and nuts, which can be offputting for unacquainted beginners. Many great wines are a harmonious cohesion of opposing elements that enable them to evolve gracefully against the rub of time, much as a diving bell's spherical shape allows it to withstand huge pressures in the depths of the ocean.

But, as Flores says, old wine is only old wine, and much of it fails to fulfil its potential — which is one of the pitfalls of the English trade's obsession with defining 'great' vintages as those deemed able to last the longest. For example, 2005 red Burgundy is the most acclaimed vintage since the turn of the millennium, with the best wines loaded with enough tannin and material feasibly to propel them, Tardis-like, far into the future. Yet, almost two decades on, many remain closed and inexpressive, with no guarantee if or when they will gloriously awaken, while other less well-regarded years have consistently provided pleasure from the outset.

Happy juice:
Dan Keeling
with González
Byass cellar
master Antonio
Flores dipping
a venencia into
a barrel of
1728 Vino Pancho
Romano, Jerez
de la Frontera.

At the top end, the still tightly wound 2005 Romanée-Conti is the most monumental union of power and weightlessness I've ever tasted, yet the younger 2007, a so-called 'off' vintage, is currently knocking it out of the park. Densely packed yet light as air, it levitates above the glass with a smoky, dried-flower sensuality, already at its apogee. Will it attain legendary status in 50 years like the 2005? I doubt it, but perhaps, like the proverbial bird in the hand, a mind-boggling mature Burgundy in the glass today is worth two 'gonna-be-greats' in the cellar. I love 'off' vintages like 2007 for joyful early drinking without the anxiety-riven guesswork of long cellaring. Indeed, my own *goût anglais* is tempered by my enthusiasm for opening fresh releases, what the French call 'drinking on the fruit', and I often find myself switching between very old and very young wines as occasion and mood dictate.

Two standouts that bookended a vertical tasting of Domaine Dujac's sainted Gevrey-Chambertin Premier Cru 'Aux Combottes' at Noble Rot Soho were a multidimensional 1978, a legendary vintage renowned for being charming from the outset, and a beautifully perfumed 2017. Indeed, 2017 red Burgundies remind me of 2007s in that, while they never generated the market excitement of siblings from 2005 and 2015/2016, drinkers don't need to wait years to begin reaping their pleasures. Bright, vivacious, friendly wines that compensate for a lack of aged complexities with the exuberance of youth, 2017s give me plenty to revel in while I agonise over how the more celebrated vintages in my imaginary room are evolving. ●

Jacques Selosse
'Substance' Blanc de Blancs
Grand Cru Brut
Champagne, France
$$$$

Marco De Bartoli
Marsala 'Superiore Oro' Riserva
Sicily, Italy
$$-$$$$

Selosse 'Substance' is the quintessential Wine from Another Galaxy, a broad-shouldered, burnished orange Blanc de Blancs aged in a solera started in 1986 to even out vintage variations and focus on the chalky Avize terroir. One critic questioned whether its Sherry-like bubbles — something vigneron Anselme Selosse developed after witnessing extended barrel-ageing in Jerez and Rioja — is a legitimate style of Champagne. But if, like me, you prioritise thrills, 'Substance' might just be your favourite Champagne of all. Selosse was among the first of the Champagne Growers to shun the region's widespread use of chemical treatments, farm living soils, and harvest smaller yields of fully ripe grapes. Having studied winemaking at Beaune's Lycée Viticole, rather than locally in Avize, he was fully dedicated to expressing terroir, rather than the Champenois' obsession with brand, when he took over his family domaine in 1978. But perhaps the most important part of Selosse's legacy will be his encouraging of other A-list growers — from Jérôme Prévost and Olivier Collin to his own son Guillaume Selosse, now at the helm of this game-changing domaine.

Say what you like about us Brits, we've got a nose for sniffing out delicious booze. And so it was in 1773 when Liverpudlian John Woodhouse discovered fortified Marsala on the western coast of Sicily and began shipping it home, where it soon became a favourite tipple of Admiral Nelson's fleet. Traditionally made with indigenous Grillo — a high-acidity grape with the potential for long ageing — using the 'il perpetuum' method, it's best served cellar temperature or slightly chilled as an aperitif or a dessert wine. Yet after two centuries of success, by the 1970s many of the Marsala cooperatives had trashed its reputation by cutting corners to increase production. Even today, Marsala is widely known mainly for cooking escalopes of veal, or making sweet zabaione, rather than something to savour in its own right. Which means you can pick up a bottle of the good stuff at a very reasonable price. The late Marco De Bartoli — a former racing car driver who grew tired of hearing people criticising Marsala — produced the best, something that his family continues. I love the spice-infused, umami-rich 1988 Marsala 'Superiore Oro' Riserva, fortified with mistella (eau-de-vie and sweet must), at the end of a meal.

Gianni Economou of Domaine Economou,
Ziros, Crete.

Domaine Economou
Oikonomoy 'Antigone' PGI
Crete, Greece
$$$

Gianni Economou is Greece's answer
to Châteauneuf-du-Pape's Château
Rayas, such are his unorthodox methods
for producing singular wines. For a
start, he says he believes in terroir
— but just not in the remote semi-
mountainous area of Ziros, Sitia,
in the far east of Crete, where
he's the only winemaker. Instead,
he sees himself as an alchemist,
perennially experimenting with native
Greek varieties such as Assyrtiko,
Thrapsathiri and Vilana in a variety
of vessels, blending oxidatively
aged cuvées into fresher ones, and
discarding those that don't work
out well into his huge store of
vinegar. Economou 'Antigone' is
made from ungrafted Liatiko (Ziros'
isolated location has kept it safe
from phylloxera), a grape previously
regarded as a workhorse variety before
he fashioned it into arguably the
Hellenic Republic's most impressive
wine. It's released ad hoc, with 2004
the latest vintage Economou deemed
ready to drink: a soulful red with a
whack of mountain herbs and a wave of
fresh acidity.

7

GREATNESS COMES FROM UNEXPECTED PLACES

Or why a superior wine from a low-ranking appellation is more gratifying than an inferior wine from a famous one

His Majesty's Government may have many (many) deficiencies, but it maintains a strong, albeit unintended, sense of irony. In June 2022, while the Duke and Duchess of Sussex were suing it over the decision to remove the couple's Metropolitan Police protection, Whitehall bureaucrats were busy awarding protection — or at least Protected Designation of Origin (PDO) — to still and sparkling wines produced in the county of their titles. When news broke that Sussex wine had become the second UK product, after Gower Salt Marsh Lamb, to be granted a PDO (roughly equivalent to France's Appellation d'Origine Contrôlée, AOC) through a new post-Brexit scheme, it was simultaneously hailed as a landmark for English wine, and derided as vacuous marketing. "Sussex wine's protected status is a joke, say Kent vineyards" ran the 16 June headline in *The Times*. And who better placed to make such an accusation than a neighbour? But protected status, as Harry and Meghan would attest, is no laughing matter. Especially as the appellation system errs toward serving the interests of the status quo, rather than those of the consumer.

Although far from the world's oldest certification, Appellation d'Origine Contrôlée began as a noble attempt to stymie widespread wine fraud in the 1920s, when lakes of North African hooch were passed off as Grands Crus to unsuspecting toffs. AOC status was first awarded in 1936 to six classifications, including Arbois and Châteauneuf-du-Pape, and still defines and polices wines according to grape varieties, the places they are grown, the size of yields harvested and, in certain areas such as

Champagne, the methods by which the wine is produced. Appellations vary in size from the Lilliputian — such as AOC Château-Grillet's idyllic amphitheatre of Viognier in the Northern Rhône — to the enormous 30,000ha of AOC Côtes du Rhône surrounding it, which contains a discombobulating 171 villages and a vast array of soils, microclimates and traditions. AOCs play an essential role ensuring winemakers operate within boundaries. Whether cheap or expensive, all great wines must taste like what they are, and where they come from, as well as offering something individual to say.

In a similar ilk, Protected Designation of Origin is said to be awarded to an area "recognised for its quality and distinctive characteristics that are exclusively a result of the geographical environment that it comes from." But can somewhere as big as Sussex have distinctive characteristics? For example, 2013 Breaky Bottom 'Cuvée Cornelis Hendriksen' — an idiosyncratic blend including Seyval Blanc, made by the maverick grower Peter Hall in the South Downs — is a delicious wine. But besides being wet, bubbly and alcoholic, it has few traits in common with bottles from larger Sussex wineries such as Rathfinny and Ridgeview. Perhaps the British government is nostalgically trying to turn back the clock to the era when appellation was an automatic signifier of style and quality, and the *carte des vins* of, say, the Dorchester Hotel, would list '1957 Nuits-St-Georges' or '1953 Volnay' without reference to domaine or grower. I'd presumed such practices went out of the window around the time that sending the kids to the corner shop to pick up 20 Marlboro became frowned upon — but I'm regularly shocked that wine lovers who should know better still buy vino based solely on its AOC.

There's nothing more conducive to complacency than a distinguished appellation — which exists to maintain the pecking order. In fact, parts of the AOC system are responsible for the bland, mediocre, technically-messed-around-with-but-commercially-acceptable hatefulness that passes its tasting panels each year, while original wines are penalised for lacking 'typicity' (ergo 'conformity'). Whether it's Dão's trailblazer Antonio Madeira — whose ambition is to promote his ancestral region but whose wines have been continually rejected by its DOC board, thus forcing him to sell them without identifying their origin — or benchmark domaines such as Trévallon, Grange des Pères, Montevertine, Soldera, Tenuta San Guido and Ferme de la Sansonnière, who have forsaken local appellations to be free of bureaucracy over the years — many of the world's most exciting wines are now classified as 'humble' Vin de France/Tavola/de Mesa/IGT/IVV etc. In the Loire Valley, a particularly high concentration of *vignerons* are working outside Appellation d'Origine Contrôlée, the myopic officiousness of which is being most conspicuously played out in AOC Quarts de Chaume.

Quarts de Chaume is the Loire Valley's sole Grand Cru, which makes its slide into obscurity more remarkable. Having been granted AOC status in 1954, today the area only produces a quarter of its purely Chenin Blanc crop in the sweet (and far less popular) style required to qualify as AOC Quarts de Chaume. The remaining 30ha is made as powerful, dry, on-trend whites typified by Domaine Belargus 'Veau' and 'Rouères', which fail AOC Quarts de Chaume's requirements and thus cannot attain Grand Cru status. Instead, they are labelled as AOC Anjou, even if dry wines express a sense of place just as well, if not arguably better in most cases, than

Breaky Bottom
(of your car):
the start of a
very long and
bumpy driveway
over the South
Downs.

Jo Pithon and
Ivan Massonnat,
Domaine Belargus,
Loire Valley.

Overleaf:
The Rock of
Vergisson,
Mâconnais.

sweet. "If something doesn't change, the historic AOC of Quarts de Chaume will die," says Domaine Belargus owner Ivan Massonnat. (Ironically, when France's regulating body INAO asked producers here to choose between being classified as a dry or sweet wine-producing AOC in 1996, they also asked the same in Savennières — whose winemakers told them where to go.) Similarly, cult-naturalista Richard Leroy started making sweet wine as AOC Coteaux du Layon, then dry as AOC Anjou, and is now Vin de France after being declined by the appellation. There are more VDF producers in the Loire than anywhere else because the system pushes them out — not that it does anything to dent demand.

Bureaucratic inertia suits lazy producers, who sell sub-par wines on outdated geographic reputations. But in Burgundy's numerous AOCs it's great to see a new model ascribing more value to the work of the *vigneron* and quality of wines than the fame of particular vineyards. The likes of Jean-Yves Bizot, who makes a coveted Pinot Noir from humble Marsannay, and Olivier Lamy, whose Domaine Hubert Lamy St-Aubin Premier Cru 'Derrière Chez Edouard Haute Densité' sells for many hundreds of pounds, epitomise the trend for elevating low-ranking terroir. While bewildering prices raise other questions about Burgundy's inaccessibility, it must be heartening for nascent producers in the region's outliers to know that they don't need vines in Chevalier-Montrachet to make a name. And even if they do own them, like 20-something Théo Dancer, they might decide that in a frost-ravaged year such as 2021, they'd like to blend Grand Cru juice with that of other Premier Cru vineyards to create 'Oskar', a chewy textured Vin de France more extraordinary than the sum of its parts. "There's value in appellations, but if a wine is good, it doesn't matter what's on the label," says Dancer.

Raising the Mâconnais

Master at
work: Jean-
Marie Guffens
in his cellar,
Vergisson,
Mâconnais.

Dancer is located in prestigious AOC Chassagne-Montrachet but releases a superb Vin de France Chardonnay and Pinot Noir from a project called Roc Breïa, based around a single 10ha block of vineyards in the hamlet of Bray in the Mâconnais. An hour's drive from the Côte de Beaune in southern Burgundy, Mâconnais wines have long been considered divisions below that of their northern neighbours — not because the region lacks world-class soils and weather, of which it clearly has both, but because history deems it so. Prices are based on confidence, and confidence relies on reputation, which becomes a self-perpetuating cycle. So, drinkers are taught that a Mâconnais St-Véran is only worth about a third of the price of a Chassagne-Montrachet, which, although St-Véran land is cheaper, means growers have to sell three times as much wine to make a comparable living. They in turn deem it necessary to cut more corners — farm using labour-saving toxins, and machine harvest much higher yields, which the appellation rules handily allow — thus producing lower-quality wines. And so it goes. Until someone either brave or crazy enough comes along and turns the system on its head.

"I always say there are three wine regions in Burgundy — two very good ones, and one in the middle that's much better known," says Jean-Marie Guffens — a.k.a. 'the crazy Belgian' — who shows no signs of either mellowing or retiring as he approaches his eighth decade. Although some of Guffens' criticisms of famous Côte d'Or names can be taken with a pinch of sulphur, his incessant skewering of the surplus of complacent family domaines clogging up its villages' backstreets is spot on. Besides, if anybody was ahead of the curve for demonstrating that it's not the appellation you are located in, but what you do with it that matters, it's Guffens and his world-beating Mâcon-Pierreclos — a lowly Mâconnais Cru that has gained renown for regularly besting top Grands Crus in blind tastings since the early 1990s. Proof that a producer's work ethic, skill and appetite for excellence matters more than their owning a famous vineyard. Of course, that's not to deny the super-eminence of terroirs such as La Romanée-Conti, where now retired co-owner Aubert de Villaine has long said his winemaking ideal is "to do nothing". But vineyards are human rather than natural constructs, and the input of a *vigneron* — no matter how restrained — contributes as much to a wine's sense of somewhereness as the climate or soils.

Around Pouilly-Fuissé, Mâconnais' best-known AOC, over 70% of the total crop is pressed at one of the many cooperatives in the area, with the must sold to *négociants* in nearby Beaujolais or the Côte d'Or. But times are changing. Just as it's now almost unbelievable that there was once a cooperative in Morey-St-Denis — now hugely desirable Côte de Nuits royalty — so the current crop of Mâconnais domaines such as Jessica Litaud, Valette, Vignes du Maynes, La Soufrandière and Guillot-Broux have erased outmoded notions that Pouilly-Vinzelles is invariably a lesser wine than a Puligny-Montrachet, or that Mâcon-Cruzille can't cut it like Meursault can. Indeed, Guffens' 2020s are among the best Burgundies I've tasted of this or any other year, as are those of Domaine Jules Desjourneys — the rivals to his Mâconnais crown. While it's easy to make a great wine in Bâtard-Montrachet, it takes a special touch to make a wine approaching the density of Bâtard-Montrachet in Pouilly-Fuissé, like Desjourneys 2020 Premier Cru 'Les Cras'.

Jessica Litaud, one of the new breed of Mâconnais producers, outside her winery in Vergisson with friend Houston. Having gained experience at domaines Guffens-Heynen and Ganevat, she makes Premier Cru Pouilly-Fuissé 'Sur la Roche' and 'Les Crays' that combine generosity and restraint.

"We came from Côte d'Or with the technique of Côte d'Or," says Fabien Duperray, one half of Domaine Desjourneys with partner Christophe Thibert, "but we wanted to make Mâconnais wine." Having represented the cream of Burgundy growers — including Domaine de la Romanée-Conti, Coche-Dury and his best friend from Beaune wine school, Arnaud Ente — as a distribution super-agent, Duperray not only has a clear idea of the kind of wine he wants to make, but insights on how to make it. Breaking the self-perpetuating negative appellation trap by seeking out old vines that produce low yields of high-quality fruit, and paying close attention to harvesting times — in a region where a few hours' extra ripening is the difference between elegant or clumsy wines — you'd be hard-pressed to pick his Chardonnays out from many others fetching hundreds or thousands of pounds. "I believe with work and knowledge you can change the rules," says Duperray. "Guffens [whom he also used to represent] told me that when he arrived here, the growers around him lacked a dream. But once you've seen his Mâcon-Pierreclos kill most Côte d'Or wines [in blind tastings], the possibilities are huge." Where you grow grapes still matters. But AOCs, PDOs, or any other bureaucratic POVs don't create wines worth falling in love with: dreamers do. ●

REWRITING THE RULES
DREAMERS ELEVATING LOW-RANKING TERROIR

Bodegas Ponce
Manchuela, Spain
$-$$

Ulysse Collin
Congy
Champagne, France
$$$$

Two hundred kilometres north-west of Benidorm lies landlocked Manchuela, one of central Spain's most exciting young DOs. Created around the millennium as a way for quality-minded producers to break away from the industrial wine-dominated La Mancha DO (which they were then part of), it's home to very old vineyards, once written off as only good enough to grow the raw ingredients for bulk wines, that are now being repurposed. Garnacha, Monastrell (a.k.a. Mourvèdre in France) and Bobal dominate the area, but while the first two have proven credentials in world-famous cuvées such as Châteauneuf-du-Pape's Château Rayas and Bandol's Domaine Tempier, the third has only started to come into its own as a 'serious' wine over the past couple of decades. Juan Antonio Ponce (pronounced "PON-thay" — not like the disparaging English word) is one of the driving forces behind Bobal's ascent. He worked with Telmo Rodríguez as part of a team covering some of Spain's most interesting winemaking projects before returning home to start his own. Finessed stony-mineral reds with good acidity, firm tannins and a herbal edge, wines such as Ponce 'P.F' are fast transforming Manchuela's reputation.

Ulysse Collin is so revered today that it's easy to forgot how challenging it was for it to start from scratch in the Coteaux du Petit Morin and Côte de Sézanne — sub-regions of Champagne few had heard of — some 20 years ago. From a bloodline of growers dating back over two centuries, Olivier Collin took back his family's vines from a long lease to Pommery in 2003 and continued selling grapes while starting to make his own wines. Following a Burgundy-inspired ethos, he's only ever made single-variety, single-vineyard cuvées in oak as opposed to non-vintage brut blends. From sumptuous 'Les Maillons' Blanc de Noirs (Pinot Noir from 50-year-old vines in Coteaux du Sézannais), to linear 'Les Pierrières' and two other extraordinary Blanc de Blancs, 'Les Enfers' and 'Les Roises' (all pure Chardonnay from the Coteaux du Petit Morin), Ulysse Collin is an example of what excellence can be achieved in historically unheralded terroirs with vision and tenacity. "The Sézannais is still quite unknown," says Olivier, "but I like being able to open the door for other local growers to say, 'This is possible'."

Renato Vezza and partner
Elisa Antonioni, Bricco Ernesto,
Roero, Piedmont.

Bricco Ernesto
Roero, Italy
$$$

To the north of world-famous Barolo good things are happening in humble Roero, like Bricco Ernesto's rich-yet-delicate Nebbiolos. Made by sometime sommelier, sushi chef, restaurant manager and motorbike mechanic Renato Vezza, Bricco Ernesto's minuscule production of red wine is classified as Vino Rosso but is more satisfying than many others in lofty local crus. "I'm a freak — I don't like to be in any DOCG, I'm just following my own rules," Vezza tells me. "Everyone said I was crazy making a wine outside of an appellation, but because I am outside I can do what I want." What Vezza wants is to make pure, no-compromises vino from the 2.5ha hillside planted with very old organically farmed vines that grandfather Ernesto left him. Before that, his father farmed it on weekends off from his job at Fiat, selling crops to a La Morra producer who had no qualms about including them in his Barolo. Drinking Bricco Ernesto Vino Rosso, a deep garnet wine with stony-fresh aromas of strawberries and rose syrup, it's easy to see why.

8

IT'S JUST BEGUN

Fresh ideas and energy in Burgundy, France

Domaine de
Cassiopée's
Talloulah
Dubourg and
Hugo Mathurin,
Maranges, Côte
de Beaune,
Burgundy.

When we say we love wine, we're always stretching the truth. What we really mean is that we love a small part of a limitless subject and, when we profess our adoration for Burgundy — the most celebrated and intricate cluster of vineyards on the planet — a fraction of that part still. Generalisations are misleading here. That a Chambolle-Musigny from a top domaine caressed your senses doesn't mean that their neighbours' won't brutalise them like a round with Mike Tyson. There are lovers and fighters everywhere. If you don't know vintage reputations, you can get caught out; here's to avoiding Chardonnay's hateful premature oxidation years — when many wines died long before their time — and so many tainted 2004 Pinot Noirs. But, as those of us who have gotten kicks from awe-inspiring, eyeball-rolling, gallop-to-the-top-of-the-nearest-mountain-and-howl-at-the-moon stupendous Burgundy can attest, falling for the wines of this part of eastern France is as undeniable as a first crush. It's an obsession only heightened by the challenges the region faces.

A landlocked agricultural zone of paysan farmers and large *négociant* houses, in Burgundy nothing ever seems to change. But of course, everything is. Average temperatures have risen by 1°C in recent years, bringing forward harvests and drought, while April frosts, which harm newly flowered vines at their most vulnerable, decimated crops in 2021, 2019, 2017 and 2016. It's hard being a grower at the best of times, let alone when no one knows how much, or how fast, the climate is changing (although prophecies that the Pinot Noir of Chambertin needs replanting with heat-loving Grenache seem premature). More immediately, *vignerons* face other

Maranges, Côte de
Beaune, Burgundy.

existential threats: chiefly death taxes at 33% of current market value when they inherit their family domaines. And if their landholdings are worth €20 million as a result of relentless rises and they don't have the cash to pay? Time to sell to a multinational or – potentially a worse fate – bring onboard shareholders who'll insist on employing oenologists to make the most deathly dull wine possible.

Land prices are reflected in bottles, although the spiralling market for Burgundy that kicked off during lockdown has calmed down. When the world went into crisis in 2020 many speculated about whether prices would drop. Remarkably, the opposite happened due to a combination of burgeoning global interest and buyers stuck at home with cash to spare. Many Grands Crus doubled or tripled in price (but have since fallen), with one merchant at the time reporting that it almost wasn't worth selling certain domaines because when they restocked, the market had risen another 10%. Of course, this wasn't instigated by the Burgundians, but largely by wealthy new buyers galvanised by social media to snap up dwindling stocks of rare vintages. In these circles, Lalou Bize-Leroy is as famous as Pablo Picasso, and drinkers are willing to pay thousands per bottle for Domaine d'Auvenay Aligoté – Burgundy's 'humble' second white grape.

Yet against this backdrop of climate change, taxes and one-percenter pricing, a more accessible side to Burgundy is blossoming. Spring frosts may be increasingly problematic, but rising temperatures have enabled vineyards in previously undesirable AOCs – such as the high slopes of the Hautes-Côtes, or Maranges, the last stop south in the Côte de Beaune – to consistently ripen grapes. Not long ago such places only grew huge yields for bulk wine, but that began changing with the arrival of aspirational young producers. "When we moved here, our neighbours asked, 'How are you going to sell 20,000 bottles of Maranges? It's not possible!'" Hugo Mathurin, who owns Domaine de Cassiopée with wife Talloulah, tells me. Certainly, their cool hillsides may have once been known for unripe fruit with rustic tannins, but savouring their silky Maranges 'Les Plantes', from 110-year-old vines, it's clear a reinvention has begun. Given that the couple learnt at the pipettes of luminaries such as Jean-Marc Roulot, Freddie Mugnier and Marie-Thérèse Chappaz, could it be any other way?

Hailing from Paris and Valence respectively, Hugo and Talloulah are typical of a new wave of outsiders re-energising Burgundy with single-minded determination. Of course, *vignerons* forging world-class reputations in less salubrious outreaches of the Côte d'Or are nothing new, from Jean-Marc Vincent in Santenay, to Sylvain Pataille's immaculate redefinition of Marsannay. Pataille's slow but inexorable rise is impressive given that he started his domaine without inherited land, but I can only imagine how much harder following a similar path would be for a *vigneronne* in Burgundy's patriarchal society. Not that Camille Thiriet, who vinifies small parcels of vines with her husband Matt Chittick, would let that stand in her way. "When I was at wine school in Beaune I was surrounded by the sons and daughters of famous winemakers," recalls Camille. "But I was still naïve and didn't realise what a challenge creating my own domaine would be. If I had known, maybe I wouldn't have done it!"

Raised in Paris, Thiriet moved to Burgundy in 2008 followed by her parents, who bought the Château de Comblanchien, the large house above the village where she was originally based, to run as a bed and

Left:
Camille Thiriet
and Yuska,
Comblanchien,
Côte de Nuits.

Right:
William Kelley
processing
fruit, Pommard,
Côte de Beaune.

breakfast. Initially producing some *cuvées* from bought-in fruit, Camille's domaine-grown Côte de Nuits-Villages reds — "an amazing, underrated and unknown appellation" — are her focus: 'Aux Montagnes', from vines she owns directly below the Château, and 'Les Retraits', located on the border with Nuits-St-Georges' famous 'Clos de la Maréchale'. In 2022 Thiriet and Chittick pulled off a coup purchasing Domaine Gilles Jourdan in Corgoloin, significantly expanding their vineyards (including the superb 'La Robignotte') and winery, and giving them the space to refine their characterful, often whole-cluster wines.

Another outsider I'm betting on for compelling wine is Englishman William Kelley. Catching his vinous infatuation at Oxford University, Kelley published his first-ever article in *Noble Rot* magazine in 2015, and has since become one of the world's most influential wine critics. This has given him unrivalled access to top *vignerons* and, long harbouring a desire to join them, he's wasted no time learning as much as possible about how the finest of wines are made. If, as he says, a winemaker needs to see the complete picture on the front of a jigsaw box before trying to put together a puzzle, he has applied an academic rigour to the entire board-game department, his Instagram feed packed with photos of rare vintages and domaines stretching back to the start of the last century.

"I want to make the kind of wines that people were making in the 1920s and '30s — wines with a big personality," says Kelley. Citing Lalou Bize-Leroy's exotic, sometimes carnal wines as the contemporary domaine closest to this style, his aim is to produce fleshy wines without heaviness with the capacity to age. Learning winemaking while also working in the symbiotic role of a wine critic is a masterstroke, providing him with time and space to hone his craft. "There are wines that I love that are slower burners, but I want to make ones where you pour it in the glass and everyone goes 'shit, what's THAT?'" he says. "I want to make wines that are dramatic and sensual — I love it when you can smell a wine across the room."

Charles Lachaux
among stake-
trained Pinot
Noir vines in
Premier Cru
'Aux Reignots',
Vosne-Romanée,
Côte de Nuits.

Dramatic and sensual are fitting descriptions for the Pinot Noirs of Arnoux-Lachaux, a long-established Vosne-Romanée domaine now under the tenure of Charles Lachaux. Like Kelley, Lachaux is an obsessive wine lover who fell under the spell of Lalou Bize- Leroy's idiosyncratic crus. Indeed, by way of explaining to his parents the style of wine that he wanted to make when he took over the family domaine — and thus the wholesale changes he wanted to implement — he poured them Leroy Savigny-lès-Beaune 'Les Narbantons' without telling them what it was. They instantly gave him their permission. Curious to find out what made Domaine Leroy wines so good and yet so different, he struck up a friendship with Lalou, which he attributes to helping him develop his philosophy rather than specific winemaking techniques. Not that he doesn't have his own quite radical ideas about those too.

It's understandable that many heirs and heiresses decide to simply continue parents' stellar work, with tiny incremental changes. But while Lachaux cites his chemist-cum-*vigneron* father Pascal's 2001s and 2002s as the wines he aims to emulate — "simple, unfiltered, pure, quite thick but textural wines" — these vintages were the exception to most others stretching back to the early '90s, when his dad hired oenologists to manipulate his wines, as many others did. Today, Charles has made controversial changes to his 14ha of prime vineyards, aiming for more harmonious fruit: replacing the conventional 'hedging' of vines (cutting off the canopies) with tressage (weaving them together to increase photosynthesis and aid ripening); no longer ploughing or cutting grass in the vineyards, to boost biodiversity; and experimenting with trellising, minimal amounts of naturally made sulphur, and doing away with oak barrels in favour of ceramic tanks.

In 2020 the effects of not ploughing radically reduced Lachaux's crop (Grand Cru Romanée-St-Vivant and Premier Cru 'Les Grands Suchots' were down to a minuscule 6hl/ha). "People don't like it when I say it's too easy in Burgundy and we have to change," says Lachaux, who suspects that some local producers do not want his revolutionary experiments to succeed. "It was good for them last year that I failed, but this year's the opposite — 'Les Chaumes' is 30–35hl/ha compared to many neighbours who were frosted, which proves it works." Theoretically, not ploughing causes vines to search deeper in soils for nutrients, producing finer, better-balanced grapes, while increased photosynthesis from the canopy promotes earlier ripening. Such changes will not take full effect for several years, but Lachaux has the conviction to stick with them while losing some of his crop. "We'll really see if it's worked in ten years' time," he says.

Thoughtful and open to ideas, Lachaux is at the vanguard of a younger generation asking what it is that makes Burgundy taste like Burgundy, rather than simply producing generic Chardonnays and Pinot Noirs that taste like they could have been grown elsewhere. Like all these winemakers, either setting up domaines or exploring fresh thoughts, Lachaux is totally immersed in his craft, but doesn't take himself too seriously. "I don't understand *vignerons* who look at their work as a chore," he says. "If they play safe and don't have fun making wine, how will others have fun drinking it?" As ever, proof can be found in the bottle, and what few bottles he actually released in 2020 have a harmoniousness, density and quality of tannin — from fine gauze in the entry-level Pinot Fin to opulent velvet in Vosne-Romanée 'Les Grands Suchots' — that will see them become classics in decades to come. ●

A SHORTCUT TO DRINKING
GREAT NEW-SCHOOL BURGUNDY

Domaine de Cassiopée
Maranges 'Les Plantes'
$$$

Domaine Camille Thiriet
Côte de Nuits-Villages 'La Robignotte'
$$$

Chanterêves
Bourgogne Aligoté 'Les Chagniots'
$$$

Domaine William Kelley
Chambolle-Musigny 'Les Fouchères'
$$$$

Domaine Arnoux-Lachaux
Nuits-St-Georges Premier Cru
'Clos des Corvées Pagets'
$$$$$

COMING UP
BURGUNDIAN WINEMAKERS TO WATCH

Domaine Thomas-Collardot
Puligny-Montrachet, Côte de Beaune
$$$

Puligny-Montrachet will forever have a place in my heart as it was an Olivier Leflaive village wine that provided my first taste of magical white Burgundy. Micro-domaine Thomas-Collardot, located in the heart of the village, is one of the newest estates that Chardonnay lovers need to know. In 2010, Jacqueline Collardot inherited Domaine Pierre Thomas from her father, producing her debut vintage five years later. Three years on, her son Matthieu began working alongside her, having studied winemaking in Beaune. Unlike neighbouring Chassagne-Montrachet and Meursault, Puligny-Montrachet has a high water table, which makes building subterranean cellars impossible, and is the reason that many domaines have historically done relatively shortened élevage in cellars above ground. Not that that stops the Collardots letting their handmade gems spend a full two winters in oak before bottling in spring, giving them time to develop body and depth. These are classically styled Puligny-Montrachets with mineral-stony details from their numerous different vineyards.

Domaine Georges Mugneret-Gibourg
Vosne-Romanée, Côte de Nuits
$$$-$$$$$

It might seem disingenuous to tip
a domaine already at the top of
the Côte d'Or as one to watch, but
now that Marion Nauleau-Mugneret
(pictured right) and Lucie Teillaud
are taking over the reins from their
mothers, small incremental changes
are increasing quality. The domaine
was founded in the 1930s, and greatly
expanded by their ophthalmologist
grandfather Georges Mugneret in the
1950s. After Georges died, it was run
by his widow Jacqueline and their
daughters Marie-Christine and Marie-
Andrée, who are now passing it on to
their own daughters, Marion and Lucie.
(The roots of Burgundy's family trees
run deep.) To be honest, I'd happily
only ever drink their overperforming
generic Bourgogne. But after a Noble
Rot tasting of several vintages of
their expansive Échézeaux, it's easy
to see the cousins doubling down
on the seriously sensual side of
Pinot Noir.

Les Horées
Beaune
$$$-$$$$

You get the sense from talking with
Les Horées' German-born Catharina
Sadde that she's only just beginning
a lifelong quest to make brilliant
Burgundy. Having already worked for
several leading domaines (including
Cécile Tremblay, Marquis d'Angerville
and Domaine de la Romanée-Conti) and
benefited from the advice of wise
friends such as Chanterêves' Tomoko
Kuriyama and Becky Wasserman, her
early vintages achieved almost instant
acclaim. A trained chef, Catharina's
love for food is as obvious as her
love for wine — a refreshing quality
given that many winemakers seem
indifferent to the link. "I like to
put a focus on humble appellations,"
she says of the 1.54ha of vineyards
she and her husband Guilhem own, as
well as farming and buying fruit from
other growers. Her Pernand-Vergelesses
Premier Cru 'Les Fichots' and
Bourgogne Rouge 'Le Vieux Sage' are
bright, pure and beautifully formed.
But perhaps her own explanation
of her ambitions for her wines —
"easily recognisable as Burgundy",
"pleasurable, easy drinking", "cheeky
but with serious foundation" — are the
best way of putting them into words.

BAD TO THE BEAUNE

Some of Burgundy's most underrated terroirs are hiding in plain sight

Rue Édouard
Fraysse,
Beaune, Burgundy.

There are plenty of things I take for granted, but being able to catch an underwater train from Central London to the beating heart of Burgundy wine in just a few hours is not one of them. Since first taking the Eurostar to Beaune with my father over 12 years ago, I have literally made it my business to return at least three times a year. Blessed with improbable numbers of wine bars, restaurants, shops and the Hospices de Beaune museum, this is a town so devoted to the pleasures of the vine that you can't throw a bunch of biodynamic Pinot Noir without hitting another foreign wine importer, or one of the horde of aspiring young *vignerons* studying at the Lycée Viticole. But although Beaune contains the third-largest number of vineyards on the Côte d'Or — after Gevrey-Chambertin and Meursault — and some historically significant terroirs, it's far less celebrated as a place where great wine is grown than the famous villages nearby.

Once upon a time, Beaune Premier Cru 'Grèves' could sell for a similar price to a Chambertin-Clos de Bèze. But its fall from the upper echelons of Burgundy wine has been profound. Perhaps the town slipped down the pecking order of drinkers' desirability because ownership of its vineyards is dominated by large domaines and merchant houses, and Burgundy these days is a region where, at least when it comes to wine, big is not beautiful. All-powerful houses like Drouhin, Jadot, Faiveley, Chanson and Bouchard Père & Fils historically controlled the fortunes of hundreds of small growers, whose livelihoods depended on them buying their crops. But by the early 20th century, many of these small *vignerons* began taking control of their own destinies by bottling and selling their wines independently. Able to finesse their work on a more modest scale—it's easier planning ideal harvesting times with fewer vineyards to worry about, for example—domaines such as Gevrey-Chambertin's Armand Rousseau and Morey-St-Denis's Ponsot made mind-bending Pinot Noirs, generating global acclaim for their appellations.

Accessing the cellars of such sainted estates is hard for winos not involved in the trade, so when in 2012 my father and I first visited Beaune we arranged tastings at the more-accessible Joseph Drouhin and Bouchard Père & Fils. Dad sadly passed away 18 months later, but I have beautiful memories of us exploring the cellars of Bouchard's 15th-century Château de Beaune, and drinking its divinely monikered flagship Beaune Premier Cru 'Grèves Vigne de L'Enfant Jésus'. Bouchard Père & Fils is the largest landholder on the Côte d'Or and was bought in 2022 by Artémis Domaines as part of a merger with Maisons & Domaines Henriot. So when I was invited to a dinner at the Château de Beaune "to go through some Bouchard bottles with a 'venerable age'" by Artémis managing director Frédéric Engerer, the thought of returning after more than a decade filled me with intrigue and nostalgia.

If anyone in the wine industry does quality on a big scale it's Artémis Domaines, from its stewardship of Bordeaux's mighty Château Latour and the Northern Rhône Valley's mystical Château Grillet (see page 209), to Burgundy's Clos de Tart and Napa's Araujo Estate Wines. While many captains of industry have business savvy but lack a personal passion for their field, Engerer combines a love for distinctive wine with an uncompromising drive to fulfil his domaines' potentials. The dinner was a rare opportunity to drink perfectly stored treasures from Bouchard's cellars with a focus on Beaune, where it is the largest vineyard owner at 50ha of nearly all Premier Cru vineyards (over three-quarters of the commune is classified as Premier Cru, with 80% planted to traditional Pinot Noir—on which I focus here).

Bouchard was renowned for some great wines in the 1940s, '50s and '60s, and I was astonished by how the ones we tasted had evolved. Burgundy suffers in some quarters from a perception that it's unable to age over long periods, and those that can are predominantly the loftiest Grands Crus. God knows, then, what business 1962 Beaune Premier Cru 'Grèves Vigne de l'Enfant Jésus' had in being so finessed and harmonious. Or 1962 Beaune Premier Cru 'Clos de la Mousse', whose rotting strawberries aromatics were so dense and alive that it's a wonder that a cork managed to hold them at bay for 60 years. Impressive too were a rustic 1942 Beaune Premier Cru 'Les Teurons', which still had fresh fruit flavours alongside a smidge of the finest Burgundian *merde*, and a delicate 1892 Beaune Premier Cru 'Grèves Vigne de l'Enfant Jésus', which put the kibosh on any suggestion that Beaune's terroir doesn't produce wines capable of evolution over many, many decades.

'Vigne de l'Enfant Jésus' is among Beaune's most famous *climats*, located in the central part of the large 'Les Grèves' vineyard. Like most Beaune Premiers Crus, 'Les Grèves' is a sunny terroir that produces refined wines with a sense of generosity and richness. Bouchard's newly released 2022 'Grèves Vigne de l'Enfant Jésus', and the even fleshier 2022 'Clos de la Mousse', hit the sweet spot for something Beaune can do so well: reds that can be enjoyed young but also have the capacity to age. Of course,

Stocks of slumbering wines in the cellars of Bouchard Père & Fils' Château de Beaune, Burgundy.

Les Horées'
Catharina Sadde
in her winery,
located a minute
walk from Beaune
train station.

generalising about Burgundy is always tricky. But the characterisation of Beaune as wine with some of the muscularity of Pommard and some of the delicacy of Volnay — but rarely reaches the heights of either — doesn't take into account recent improvements. Certainly, Domaine des Croix's 2017 Beaune Premier Cru 'Les Grèves', grown close to 'Vigne de l'Enfant Jésus', proves that sensational vino can be made here in the right hands.

Loire-born David Croix of Domaine des Croix typifies a generation of *vignerons* eking magic from Burgundy's humbler appellations. Like, say, Sylvain Pataille in Marsannay, Croix's roster of well-defined Premiers Crus have become new-school benchmarks, from the tenderness of afore-mentioned 'Les Grèves' to the dense, bulging biceps of 2020 Premier Cru 'Pertuisots'. (If another cliché of Beaune is that of it being fruity easy drinking, this is the antithesis — I'd love to revisit this wine in decades' time.) Greatly improving farming and refining a gentle style of winemaking since his first Beaune vintage in 2005, Croix is lighting the way for rising stars such as Chanterêves, Thomas Bouley and Catharina Sadde, who are already making great wines in tiny quantities here. "I'd like to buy more land in Beaune. Because people don't have a fixed image of it, you can surprise them," says Sadde, who makes a fabulous 'Les Prévolles' and whose Les Horées project is one of the hottest on the Côte d'Or. It's these tenacious small producers who have the power to help restore Beaune's reputation as a place where amazing wines are grown as much as they are sold or drunk — if only they can get their hands on more vineyards to do so. ●

Domaine des Croix
Beaune Premier Cru 'Pertuisots'
$$$

Domaine Jean-Marc et Thomas Bouley
Beaune Premier Cru 'Les Reversées'
$$$

Domaine Michel Lafarge
Beaune Premier Cru Grèves
$$$

Domaine Fanny Sabre
Beaune 'Clos des Renardes' Rouge
$$$

Les Horées
Beaune 'Les Prévolles'
$$$$

Bouchard Père & Fils
Beaune Premier Cru
'Grèves Vigne de l'Enfant Jésus'
$$$$

Joseph Drouhin
Beaune Premier Cru 'Clos des Mouches'
Blanc
$$$$

10

THE IGNOBLE ART OF BLIND TASTING

Or how trying to name an unidentified wine can chop your ego down to size

Ain't fine wine a tease? The more you learn, the more you realise there are endless intricacies that you'll never understand. And if at any time you need this reaffirming, to have it hammered home, as if set upon by a gang of deranged sommeliers, there's nothing like 'blind tasting' — a.k.a. trying to identify a wine without seeing the label — to give your ego a trim. Think that's a '90s Bordeaux in the glass? Close... it's '70s Rioja. Are you sure this is a famous Chenin Blanc? Not a chance — it's a village Meursault. Or perhaps you're confident you can always spot Pol Roger's telltale characteristics from 100 paces. Bad luck, chum, this is one of those infernal English sparklers you've been slagging off to whoever will listen. Yeah, there are good reasons why professional critics are hesitant to embarrass themselves in this kind of parlour game. Like the time Mâconnais iconoclast Jean-Marie Guffens served Robert Parker 1986 Mouton Rothschild — which Parker had previously awarded 100 points — and the critic called it a $10 Californian Cabernet Sauvignon. At least he got the grape right.

To be fair to Parker (believe me, I feel his pain), this is a particularly brutal example of the type of rogering that a blind tasting can administer, which even the best tasters sometimes have to grin and bear. But the fact that it happened to wine's most successful influencer (LONG before the term was co-opted by vacant Instagram-nutjobs), largely responsible for contemporary criticism's obsession with 'objectivity' — you've also gotta laugh. Some of my best drinking pals are also 'objectivists' — fantasists who can't relax unless they're a) serving a mystery white that costs 20 quid that they think you could mistake for Montrachet, thus proving you've no idea what you're talking about; or b) committing the vinous equivalent of a Harrow school 'de-bagging', stripping a venerable cru of context (philosophy, typicity, point in its evolution, etc) so that it may be judged 'impartially'. But while seeing a famous label makes people more positively disposed to a wine, on the other hand I find that blind tasting makes them more focused on deficiencies. Besides, drinking wine like a NORMAL FUCKING HUMAN BEING doesn't mean we're all so easily influenced that we can't compensate for our biases.

That's not to say the odd round of 'Guess Who?' isn't entertaining — in a similar way to how 17th-century peasants found public executions a hoot — or, in a professional context, a useful way of appraising bottles (we chose our restaurants' house Vinho Verde 'Chin Chin' from blind tasting a short list of ten candidates). This kind of tasting is a variation on a theme: if 'double-blind' is knowing nothing about a wine, 'single-blind' might mean knowing its region, vintage or producer. Twice a year the Southwold trade tasting group assesses Cru Classé Bordeaux four and ten years on from harvest, grouping châteaux in sub-regions to avoid comparing apples and oranges. Likewise, *Noble Rot* magazine's Champagne versus English sparkling tastings have produced great insights into how both are evolving. But the fact is that all blind tastings can be skewed to produce a desired result. Even 1976's 'Judgement of Paris' — when Californian wine (typically fruit-forward) famously aced First Growth claret (typically requiring more age to be at its best) — was to objectivity what Stig of the Dump was to interior design.

So, are great blind tasters born or can they be made? Any sommelier worth their Sauternes follows a boozy Code of the Samurai that requires total dedication, conscientiously abstaining from consuming both very hot and very cold food and drink in case they negatively affect their palate. Like prize fighters in training for a championship bout, their way to the top is by repeatedly tasting and serving the world's greatest wines in a busy restaurant setting. "Getting good at blind tasting is about repetition," says renowned ex-sommelier-turned-Californian *vigneron* Raj Parr. "I haven't worked the floor in years so my edge is gone, but in my heyday my confidence was so high that I'd challenge anyone to give me any classic wine blind, and feel I'd nail it." That's no hyperbole; I've served Parr — the best taster I know — 50-year-old Burgundies that he's narrowed down to appellation, vintage and producer. An impressive and, for the rest of us, dispiriting skill — especially when repeated on three or four mystery wines in a row.

Like most other mortals my own blind-tasting success-to-failure ratio is skewed, like a hippo on a seesaw, towards the latter. But that's not to say my few notable successes — identifying Domaine d'Auvenay Aligoté from the list at Beaune's Maison du Colombier in front of a table of somms by recognising its popcorn signature, or picking vintages of Château Haut-Brion from their telltale warm brick aromas — aren't up there with the birth of my children as the happiest moments of my life. But, more seriously, hoping to identify a mystery wine by its odour and flavours alone — which change over time and can be manipulated through winemaking — leaves a huge margin for error. The most effective strategy is to focus on the elements of grape varieties that don't change; i.e. the acid 'structure' (level, shape) of white wines, and tannic structure of reds, which are both felt in the mouth. For example, Sangiovese has moderate-to-high levels of sandy tannins felt on the gums rather than on the tongue, and if a wine smells like Riesling, but has low acidity, it's likely to be something else (read *Beyond Flavour* by ex-Cambridge University blind-tasting team member Nick Jackson MW for more on this).

Of course, an analytical approach isn't for everyone, and if you know your fellow imbibers well, you can play the player, not the game. A friend had wonderful things to say about me when I nailed his 1978 Château de Beaucastel without even smelling the glass at an annual Christmas lunch (I'd remembered he'd bought the same wine two years previously and thought it worth a punt), while another pal has no more than ten favourite producers in his cellar, one of which he always brings. But as interesting new wine regions have sprung up around the globe over the past decade, with *vignerons* sharing ideas and techniques on comparable soils, stylistic differences between, say, a Ribeira Sacra Mencía, a Sonoma Coast Syrah and a Côte-Rôtie can be diminished. This, however, can also be a good thing: with prices spiralling you may not be able to afford Coche-Dury Meursault, but you might find a cheaper wine that reminds you of it elsewhere (try Dominio del Águila Viñas Viejas blanco from Ribera del Duero, see page 127).

Blind tasting sure isn't easy, and I've even seen Raj Parr caught out once or twice, despite the fact that his supernatural senses are allied to a deep knowledge—the other essential ingredient for being a good taster. This is illustrated by his process for once deducing that a mystery red poured for him by Aubert de Villaine of Domaine de la Romanée-Conti was 1948 Grands Échézeaux. "Aubert said, 'I'll give you one hint—this vintage is not well known, and it came after a great year'," says Parr. "Although the '37s were good I couldn't imagine it was as old as '38. Thinking of another great vintage—1959—I wondered whether it could be a '60. But the '60s I'd had were lean and high acid. So, coming after the great 1947, and even though I'd never had a 1948 red Burgundy before in my life, '48 seemed the right answer. And it had that coffee, cola tone that Grands Échézeaux develops after a few years." Parr gets closer than most to mastering the art of blind tasting, but I'd much rather spend my time focusing on what makes a wine special, and how it makes me feel, than trying to name what it is. Wine connects man, time and nature like nothing else; why wouldn't you take it all into account? ●

11

WHO'S AFRAID OF ROMANÉE-CONTI?

The anxiety and the ecstasy of the world's most fabled wine

Romanée-Conti vineyard, Vosne-Romanée, Burgundy.

Top Grand Cru Burgundy has some claims to becoming a lost genre of wine. The primary aim of Burgundy is to provide sensual pleasure; the present-day role of its rarest, most venerated bottles seems to me to be to assure the very wealthy that they are drinking—just as they are eating, driving, flying and screwing—the very best that money can buy. No one else can afford to drink it. Not the doctors, the dentists, the lawyers, the architects or the salt-of-the-earth arms-dealers who, up until a few years ago, were assured of occasional access to the rarefied upper echelons of the Côte d'Or. But when the first thing that anybody mentions when they talk about Romanée-Conti—the world's most fabled wine—isn't its historic pedigree, its aromatic and textural sophistication, or its ability to rouse mountain-top moments of spiritual ecstasy, but the price—you know that something has gone awry. So let's get it out of the way. At £20,000 per 750ml bottle on the open market, Romanée-Conti is no ordinary fermented fruit juice.

I assume all wine lovers have their own fantasies about unattainable bottles like Romanée-Conti. We drink them, in our heads—and they transform from earthbound libations into fairy tales. When I first started building a cellar in 2010, Burgundy still ran second to Bordeaux in price and demand. While leading producers' Grands Crus commanded substantial tariffs, they could also be occasionally justified to provide special insights. I remember one evening cooking one of my favourite wine-centric dishes, braised quails with peas, drinking '08 JF Mugnier Musigny—a vineyard that vies with Romanée-Conti as the Côte de Nuits' most legendary—and becoming joyously, drunkenly, serenely aware of how it shifted form in the kitchen candlelight. A momentous revelation, I felt as if I'd rocketed into space, pressed my face against the window, and found a new perspective on everything below. Now that same bottle, bought then for £400, sells for over £2,500 — what hope does a thrill-seeker have of satisfying their curiosity about the view from the top?

At least we can all comfort ourselves with the fact that a more diverse array of profound yet affordable wines is being grown around the world today than ever before. The Gredos Mountains, Rheinhessen, Naoussa, Brunello di Montalcino — authenticity is far from the preserve of La République. But at the other end of the spectrum there's still a peculiar inverse-snobbery that exists about paying for quality artisanal vino — especially considering the environmentally harmful methods used to make industrial plonk. Laying out on Champions League tickets, luxury holidays and theatre seats are experiences widely agreed to be a worthy use of money. Yet spending similar amounts rewarding real people who have got into considerable debt to farm vines without toxins at the mercy of hailstorms and spring frosts, harvest by hand, vinify, store, bottle, market and sell their dream wines without compromise? Perish the thought.

Romanée-Conti is a myth as much as a pure Pinot Noir, and 1.814ha of the most-coveted real estate on the planet. Access to it has got only marginally better since 1760, when the Prince de Conti bought what was already considered Burgundy's supreme vineyard, reserving its full production to serve to guests at his lavish beanos. Today, as then, its reputation as wine's GOAT remains undiminished by the inaccessibility of the 5,000 to 9,000 bottles it produces per year. Unlike Bordelais superstars such as Château Latour — whose production runs into six figures — Romanée-Conti's aura is such that wine geeks genuflect in its presence. But to be fair to the domaine it goes out of its way to share its heritage with a few of those drinkers who would appreciate it the most. Even if attending its coveted annual tasting at the Thames-side offices of Corney & Barrow, its UK importer, can feel like gate-crashing a coffee morning at Eton College.

"'Nothing at times is more expressive than silence,' George Eliot (1819–1880). We ask that you taste in silence," reads a sign next to the table from which the domaine's Grands Crus are being poured. Around the basement tasting room, a variety of journalists, sommeliers and merchants perch or stand examining thimble-sized pours of wines that they cannot afford to drink, doing their best not to have too good a time lest they be told to be quiet. Such reverence seems strangely out of sync with how so much about wine culture has become more informal. But credit where credit is due. Assured of selling its Montrachet, Corton-Charlemagne, Corton, Vosne-Romanée Premier Cru 'Duvault-Blochet', Échézeaux, Grands-Échézeaux, Romanée-St-Vivant, Richebourg, La Tâche and Romanée-Conti several times over, the domaine doesn't need to conform to trends. The tasting is simply an expression of its generosity and desire to pass on the flame.

There are many things that can be gleaned from such meagre pours of nascent Burgundies. For a buyer their colour, clarity, acidity, sweetness, tannin, length and harmony say much about their quality, and how they may evolve. But unlike drinking it — attentively following it in a relaxed environment alongside the natural context of food while the benevolent effects of alcohol take hold — you don't get to know it. Like a clip of a song, or the highlights of a sporting event, the experience lacks emotion. And the more complex the wine, the hollower still. When I think back to my earliest wine revelations, they resonate with shapes, colours and sensations — not value judgements. I can still see my first-ever Condrieu metamorphose into a three-dimensional Rubenesque fleshpot after 30 minutes in the glass, and the vivid, deep royal blue of Ridge Monte Bello. The idea that wine can transport you — to clear ponds, woods and gullies, shorelines of salty sea air and balmy stone streets — is missing from a tasting. And although I had sampled several young Romanée-Contis at the tasting and domaine, I never dreamt I'd actually be able to drink the ultimate yardstick with which to measure all other wines.

Right:
The famous stone cross demarcating the southern end of Romanée-Conti.

Overleaf:
AOC Romanée-Conti outlined in white.

The Wisdom of Olney

When the American writer Richard Olney described the events of 28 March 1991 as "a voyage never taken before and one which can never be repeated" in his venerable volume *Romanée-Conti*, he was only partially right. Having been commissioned to write THE book on the world's most fabled wine, he led a panel of six luminaries tasting 45 vintages of Romanée-Conti, several of which were the last bottle in the domaine's cellars, which even the co-directors Aubert de Villaine and Lalou Bize-Leroy had never tried. (The other guests were Sotheby's Serena Sutcliffe, Christie's Michael Broadbent, and critic Michel Bettane). The wines, which had matured in ideal conditions and never suffered the trauma of long-distance transportation, were served in flights from the 1980s to 1915. Descriptions of these Romanée-Contis in Olney's book read as close to sensual nirvana as it's possible to get without divine intervention. But, as I say, he was only partially right. Because on 4 April 2022, de Villaine, assisted by the filmmakers Franck Ribière and Vérane Frédiani, organised a similar event for a new edition of the book — centred, by necessity, on the past 25 vintages of Romanée-Conti.

I never met Richard Olney, whose life was toasted with jeroboams of La Tâche at a wake at his Provençal home in 1999, but his teachings have profoundly influenced my tastes. Besides *Romanée-Conti* he also wrote the definitive book *Yquem* — widely considered the planet's greatest sweet wine — as well as *The French Menu Cookbook* and Time Life's cookery series, which he edited. But it was his indirect influence on two protégés that has most informed my way of thinking: Simon Hopkinson, whose *Week In Week Out* helped me learn how to cook, and Kermit Lynch, whose *Adventures on the Wine Route* made me consider wine from a fresh perspective, inspiring me to leave a career signing artists to record companies for a métier as an importer, restaurateur and writer. I particularly related to Olney and Lynch's love of wine as drinkers — not academics — and their joyous celebrations of long-aged traditional styles.

Although Lynch — an importer responsible for popularising numerous French winemaking greats in the States — had never been Domaine de la Romanée Conti's agent, he'd long been friends with its soon-to-retire co-director Aubert de Villaine from working with him on his personal Bouzeron estate. So, while Ribière and Frédiani had, quite unbelievably at the time, invited me to the tasting of a lifetime, it was Uncle Kermit who helped rubber-stamp my pass with de Villaine when finalising the eight-person guest list to what would be his career swan song. In Burgundy you can taste wine at domaines, but you cannot usually buy or drink it there — no matter who you are. And considering the value of the bottles, a place at the table was gold. Indeed, for a Burgundy lover, complimentary access to 25 Romanée-Contis felt like being beamed backstage at 25 of Bowie's greatest gigs. As the critic Michel Bettane — the only member of the original 1991 event at the re-run besides de Villaine — later told me: "No one — no super-rich collectors — could do what we are about to do. A vertical of DRC wines — yes. But 25 vintages of authentic Romanée-Conti, and the ability to replace a corked bottle? Not a chance."

The weeks leading up to the tasting seemed to grind on for years. Above all, I longed to drink Romanée-Conti as the highest reference point with which to measure all other wines. But I was anxious that Covid would can-

cel the event, or that I'd arrive with a blocked nose from a common cold and be unable to smell. When the day finally came to travel down to Burgundy, check into Vosne-Romanée's Le Richebourg Hotel, and visit the domaine's old offices on Rue Derrière le Four for a pre-tasting dinner, it felt like the end of term, it felt like Christmas morning, it felt illegal, it felt great. Anyone who's wondered if the showboating of modern 'icon' commercial wineries is inversely related to the quality of the wine that they produce need only see here for affirmation. Last decorated several decades ago with flock wallpaper, antique radiators and washed-out photos of past harvests, this is the dining room of a working winery, not a global luxury brand.

Waxing lyrical about a Pinot Noir that costs far more than many people's salary may be as socially acceptable as a facial tattoo of a tarantula. But 1937 Romanée-Conti is an auspicious start to any meal. Light brown, like a 200-year-old Madeira, its delicate perfume of fading rose petals, caramel and spice combines with an unctuous yet weightless texture and a blood orange-like acidity, freshening the senses like a sprinkler on a late summer lawn. "This tastes of the real domaine," coos de Villaine in his measured manner of speaking, welcoming all with an aperitif with the twang of eternity. Around him stand his successors as co-directors, Perrine Fenal and Bertrand de Villaine; Michel Bettane and fellow critic Allen 'Burghound' Meadows; John Olney, the nephew of Richard Olney and winemaker at Ridge Vineyards; and Paz Levinson, Anne-Sophie Pic's head sommelier. And me, with Franck Ribière and Vérane Frédiani filming proceedings.

Grown on pre-phylloxera rootstock before the increasingly unproductive vineyard was replanted in 1947, 1937 Romanée-Conti is our only glimpse of the hallowed cru until the following morning.

(1945 Romanée-Conti, of which 600 bottles were made, holds the record as the most expensive bottle of wine ever sold, raising $558,000 in New York in 2018.) Instead, dinner continues with 2019 Corton-Charlemagne, the domaine's opulent new white *cuvée* that sticks to the tongue like Velcro and has the clarity of spring water; an intoxicating, super-floral 2008 Romanée-St-Vivant; and a 1979 Grands-Échézeaux that smells like dried raspberries, celery and brambles, and has a silken texture under a mottled patina of time. Can Romanée-Conti possibly better these? I'd marinate myself in any of them until they rolled out my senseless body, drunk on the vapours of paradise, into the gutters of Vosne-Romanée. "Appreciating a great Romanée-Conti requires a different mind-set and a certain effort on the part of the drinker," wrote Allen Meadows in *The Pearl of the Côte*, a book that left me despondent about the wine's inaccessibility many years ago. Likewise, former domaine co-director Lalou Bize-Leroy once said it took her 20 years to understand why Romanée-Conti is its greatest vineyard. What hope do I have in one day?

Part of the
first flight of
Romanée-Conti —
2002, 2001 and
2000.

The Vapours of Paradise

"*Est-ce que tout le monde est prêt à parler des vins*?" de Villaine's voice snaps me out of my glass and back into the room. I'm not ready to talk about the wines. I may never be. And not only am I NOT READY, I'm free-falling like a parachutist twisted up in expectations, not knowing which way is up and which is down. It's 10.30am the next morning and eight of us are sat around a table in the Prince de Conti's *cuverie* on Rue de la Goillotte, a bright, open room, free from all adornment save for two other tables, laid with flights of Romanée-Conti. "Dan, are you ready?" de Villaine asks again. Forty-five minutes have vaporised since we began tasting. Forty-five weeks would be more appropriate to grasp the first flight of, as I'm now realising, not just the world's most fabled, but notoriously hard to decipher wine. I try finding my bearings, searching for Pinot's lodestar of ripe fruit. Yet vegetal smells of the vineyard overwhelm me — damp woodland, sappy shoots, and faint echoes of rose. Michel Bettane begins appraising '97 to '04 vintages *en français*. It's not so bad being the only person with lousy French in the room if it means I have more time contemplating the wines before taking my turn in the spotlight — although it would be nice not to contradict everyone else.

Whether Breton or Cornish, wine appreciation's canon of worn adjectives — creamy, peppery, minerally — is woefully inadequate, but especially so when applied to the undisputed champion of Burgundy. Zappa famously once said that writing about music made as much sense as dancing about architecture, but here I am again with my blunt pencil trying to draw a smell. So, are we to blame for attempting to describe the ineffable, or is it the magic of vino itself? If it wasn't for the happiness it provides, the anxieties it allays, and the foods it enhances, there definitely would be more rationale doing the breaststroke about Cabernet Franc. But this is no time to despair about the limits of language! Focus on each wine's texture, its layers of aroma and flavour, its harmony and finesse, and find some honest insights. Besides, I'm certain most people are more interested in hearing about how a wine might make them feel than what it tastes like. And the way these first Romanée-Contis fuse Bourguignon grunt with celestial finesse is like nothing I've ever experienced.

Anticipation has been replaced by a shot of adrenaline straight into the olfactory nerve and the demons that wine fosters — do I really know my stuff? — are trying to weigh me down. I check the wines' colours and raise each glass to my nose in turn and inhale. I take a sip and roll it around my mouth focusing on the acidity, texture, sense of energy and length of time that it lingers on my taste buds, and repeat. Then the shock sets in. Every time I put my nose back in a glass the wine inside has changed. The '02 and '04 are far more vegetal than I ever expected. Perhaps they need time to understand — something I resolutely do not have. I berate myself for not instantly appreciating the '97 and '98, but sensing a jump in quality with the monolithic '99, I ruthlessly discard both and push on. It's like winning first-class tickets on the *Titanic* only to then have to choose which of your kids to put in the lifeboats as the ship goes down.

Romanée-Conti's vegetal characteristics come in part as the result of whole bunches of grapes being used in fermentation rather than first being stripped of their stems. The domaine has long been at the vanguard of Burgundian wineries (along with Leroy, Arnoux-Lachaux and Dujac)

that include stems to develop aromatic and textural complexity, losing colour but gaining freshness. In contrast, legendary *vigneron* Henri Jayer insisted that including whole bunches led to green flavours. But Burgundy is no longer a marginal climate where grapes struggle to ripen, and Romanée-Conti's exquisite perfumes and tannins become ever more intoxicating. Soon, vintage characteristics come into focus. The '01 makes me feel as if I'm under the vines with my nose pressed into the roots. Akin to a concentrated essence of Burgundy – decaying strawberries, rose petals and cow shit (a theme throughout the day) – it's as dense as mercury but as light as air. Likewise, the exotic '00 and '03 – critically underrated 'warm' years – have incredible proportions and finesse. Are the wines finally opening up – or is it me? Here was weep-sweet-tears-of-ecstasy-while-angels-sing-hallelujah Romanée-Conti in its full glory.

If getting my head around the first flight of wines was the olfactory challenge of my life, the second is the mother lode, my pleasure receptors working overtime to keep up with the onslaught. A vineyard is a barcode-like mixture of climate, soils, exposure and drainage running throughout different years, allied to the numerous profound decisions a *vigneron* makes in each cycle. In Romanée-Conti themes repeat, and the completeness of the wines from '05 to '12 is obvious. Monumental density is delivered with magical ethereality, producing harmonious wines. Although there are winemaking methods for producing prominent fruit, there's no way to manufacture Romanée-Conti's natural concentration and textural sophistication. It's a sophistication that seems like simplicity – which, allied to an ability to remain youthful against the rub of time, is the closest I can get to a pithy definition of what constitutes 'great' wine.

The 4 April 2022 tasting (clockwise from bottom left): Bertrand de Villaine, John Olney, Dan Keeling, Perrine Fenal, Paz Levinson, Michel Bettane, Aubert de Villaine.

'05 Romanée-Conti gives me goose bumps. An intense perfume of far-off bonfires and Chinese spices frames a structured wine with a weighty texture that somehow seems to float. It's only beginning to reveal its wonders and should still be at its apogee in 75 years, when the only people who'll be able to afford to drink it will be asteroid-mining tycoons. '10 Romanée-Conti is floral, animal and seductive. It's more transparent than its siblings, but just as finessed and spherically shaped in the mouth, demanding serious cellar time to fulfil its huge potential. By contrast, the '07 is peaking now, its sublime fragrance levitating high above the glass. It's hard to believe that this actually originated in grapes. Robust yet open and light as air, it's svelte and alive, with a meaty, smoky, dried flower-like sensuality. I doubt the '07 has the staying power to reach immortal status like the '05 and the '10. But right here, right now, it's everything you could wish for.

The '11 melds white flowers with signature rose petals and spice, trumping the year's tricky growing conditions, while the killer '12 delivers more of those sensual vineyard aromas. Likewise, '08 is a wine that I'd love to linger over for a whole day — if it wasn't time for lunch. We adjourn like gamblers on winning streaks. "I've bad news," de Villaine tells me. "There's no wine, to keep us sharp. But there's always something sad about a meal with no wine." After lunch, we walk up Rue de Temps Perdu, past lonesome blossoms to the weathered old stone cross demarcating the southern end of Romanée-Conti. Roughly 150 by 150 metres, this visually unremarkable patch of land lies precisely mid-slope with perfect drainage and all-day exposure, its topsoil of pebbles and sandy clay covering limestone and marl formed by fossilised oysters. Legions of naked vines in greens and browns line up the slope to the forest on the hilltops, from where the wind comes howling down into the village.

Anyone looking for affirmation of climate change need only note the rising ripeness levels of Romanée-Conti over the past 25 years. Unlike the last flight, which made me wonder if ten to 15 years is the perfect time to begin broaching Romanée-Conti, '13 to '21 is more of an intellectual than hedonistic pursuit. The '15's strawberry-raspberry scent is so vivid I almost visualise the bloom on the freshly picked berries, while the monumental '18 has so many layers of smoke and flowers, and so much depth. '20 levitates on the palate — a future classic, just like the far svelter, swashbuckling-musketeer-in-the-making '21. As many winos can attest, the last glass is often the best, and as the tasting winds down, and others compare the vintages en français, I return to my half-drunk set of wines. There's over half a million quid's worth of BONA FIDE ROMANÉE-CONTI left around the room. So wotcha gonna do?

Vive La Différence

I wonder how many drinkers have sought out Romanée-Conti looking for more: more power, more fruit, more complexity — and been left disillusioned by its restraint. But just like, say, writing or cooking, 'more' doesn't necessarily mean 'better'. If anything, Romanée-Conti's genius lies in its completeness. Is it worth the money? Perhaps that depends on your personal tastes, your experience of enigmatic wines, and how many state-owned assets you siphoned off during the fall of the USSR. But the price of top Grand Cru Burgundy undoubtedly distorts the idea of what wine is made for, and is by far the biggest obstacle to it being drunk and legends living on.

I return home the day after the tasting feeling like an astronaut who's walked on the moon. I may never drink Romanée-Conti again, but knowing what it's like makes a difference to how I think about the wines that I can. Great wine should be for everyone, not just the wealthy. But while Romanée-Conti, Musigny et al. are only accessible to the 0.01%, we can all console ourselves with the fact that, thanks to improved farming and growing temperatures (one of the very few positives of climate change), now is the best time ever to discover beautiful wines elsewhere. Besides, traditional wine culture has never been about being the 'greatest' per se, but celebrating difference. Or, put more simply, *vignerons* making the best wines possible from where their grapes grow as an expression of individuality and love. ●

Domaine Jacques-Frédéric Mugnier
Chambolle-Musigny Premier Cru
'Les Amoureuses'
Burgundy, France
$$$$$

If aliens land and ask what makes wine so special I'd open a bottle of Frédéric Mugnier Chambolle-Musigny Premier Cru 'Les Amoureuses', from a mystical vineyard in the next village to Romanée-Conti. 'Les Amoureuses' is Pinot Noir at its most ethereal — a criminally overused wine descriptor, but completely spot on for Mugnier's top crus. His 2008 is one of my favourite-ever bottles, a light-coloured red that looks more like a dark rosé with a sensuality far beyond most mortal wines. Likewise, Mugnier's cashmere-textured 2000 Grand Cru Musigny operates on some kind of higher frequency, its sublime perfume constantly shifting form in the glass.

It's been said that aspiring vignerons would be better studying philosophy than oenology to help wines fulfil their potential, and perhaps in the future Mugnierism — or, specifically, Mugnier's thoughtful approach to winemaking — will be taught in school. Indeed, he acts as if it's his job to simply avoid fouling up what his vines produce every year, striving to remove elements that obscure the quality of the fruit. I'm sure those elements include himself, of which he'd happily remove all trace. All Mugnier's vines are processed with uncompromising integrity in the same way every year to transparently express the terroir and vintage. Similarly to Romanée-Conti, great vintages of 'Les Amoureuses' and 'Musigny' have a sophistication than seems like simplicity, like a centuries-old melody or song.

Case Basse di Gianfranco Soldera
Toscana IGT
Tuscany, Italy
$$$$

It may be harder than ever to
reconcile the price of many wines with
value. But once you consider the love
that Gianfranco Soldera lavished on
his Sangiovese, you might consider
selling a kidney a small price to
pay in order to wallow in some of the
greatest Italian reds ever made. Chez
Soldera, there were no compromises.
There was no second best. Routinely
producing 15,000 bottles from a
crop that others would stretch to
50,000, methods such as discarding
first-class grapes that didn't fit
a uniform size and using only free-
run juice may seem as eccentric
as some of his proclamations (my
favourite was when he told Jancis
Robinson that the French didn't have
good soils and would be "better off
growing potatoes"). Until you taste
the wines, that is. Pure, delicate,
rich, original, exotic: words don't
do Soldera's former Brunello di
Montalcinos justice (he fell out with
the consorzio and left the appellation
in 2013), but you might try imagining
Richebourg ripened by Mediterranean
sunbeams. Even if, unlike centuries-
old Richebourg, he planted his
vineyards from scratch: something else
that blows my mind. Soldera was a
self-made genius whose Sangiovese is
a benchmark for generations to come.

Stella di Campalto, Podere San Giuseppe
Brunello di Montalcino
Tuscany, Italy
$$$$

If any winemaker is the stylistic
heir to Gianfranco Soldera, it's
Stella di Campalto. Originally
from Rome, di Campalto was gifted
the Podere San Giuseppe estate in
Castelnuovo dell'Abate, Tuscany, as a
wedding present from her ex-husband's
family. A teetotaller at the time,
she didn't know what to do with it.
But after discovering the EU was
offering large grants for planting new
vineyards, she set about establishing
4ha of vines with a view to renting
them out. Four years later, just as
she was about to sign them away to
another producer, she had a change
of heart and decided to ferment her
debut harvest instead. Inspired by
drinking the finessed, traditionalist
in purezza Sangioveses of Soldera
and Poggio di Sotto, rather than
overwrought modernist Brunellos, she
has been perfecting her intoxicating
style — a sensual blend of rose
petals, strawberries and earth —
ever since.

12

WHITE SHIFT

*Chassagne-Montrachet's profound
generational change*

The derelict
Abbaye de
Morgeot,
Chassagne-
Montrachet,
Burgundy.

Perhaps the Burgundy backlash is in the post. God knows, it's not hard to imagine drinkers becoming disillusioned by the seemingly irrepressible rise — and demands — of one of La République's most prestigious wine regions (bon voyage, Bordeaux). But what makes the Côte d'Or different, so irresistible and fascinating is that it's an endlessly layered microcosm of the world at large. Sure, there's big business — the distastefully expensive bottles and archaic hierarchies aiding its lazier brethren to prosper through inertia. Yet Burgundy is also in an exciting period of change: of innovative farming methods; of the realisation that a *vigneron*'s sensibilities are just as, if not more, important than the historical reputations of famous terroirs. And for all the destruction that climate change threatens to inflict in the future, right here and now rising temperatures are invigorating crus and sub-regions previously often too cool to ripen grapes.

Of course, a new generation is driving such changes. And what a brilliant bunch they are. First there's an influx of inspired foreigners drumming up interest in their nascent *cuvées*. Then, the young blood being stirred by the passing of the baton at many established domaines. For yes, you might picture what kind of reprobate that arch-outsider Jean-Marie Guffens is alluding to when he says, "You generally don't find great wines made by estates that are passed from father to son. Some of them go so far back I call them 15 de-generations." But exceptions prove the rule, and heir-visionaries such as Charles Lachaux, and Mugneret-Gibourg daughters Marion and Lucie are raising the bar in their Vosne-Romanée domaines — while in Chassagne, an extensive generational shift is afoot.

Back in the early 19th century the good *vignerons* of Chassagne-Montrachet were devotees of the old Gallic creed that 'the first duty of a wine is to be red'. But by the late 1980s, that started to change as growers extensively replaced Pinot Noir with Chardonnay due to its potential for higher yields and the popularity of white wines from neighbouring Puligny-Montrachet and Meursault. Although quality has now rocketed in nearby appellations such as St-Aubin, for decades the ambrosial Chardonnays of these three villages were unsurpassed.

In terms of numbers of A-list producers Meursault has historically been the master of all. Sure, Puligny is home to the world-beating Leflaive, while Chassagne has the revered Ramonet. But it was Meursault's crop of superstar domaines – Coche-Dury, Roulot, Lafon and Ente – that have always had the world in their *tastevins*. Don't get me wrong, they still do. But Chassagne is the village increasingly on winos' lips, with numerous zoomers taking over estates. As 20-something Mathis Colin – who, with younger brother Clément, is assuming control at the domaines of parents Pierre-Yves Colin-Morey and Caroline Morey – says: "Chassagne may not be the Côte de Beaune's benchmark name but the wines speak for themselves. When you drink old Ramonet there's no gap in quality with Coche-Dury."

Coche-Dury has been responsible for some of the most astonishing vinous highs of my life: intense, deep, satin-textured whites with signature 'struck-match' aromas. Similar aromatics are also a hallmark of Pierre-Yves Colin-Morey Chassagne-Montrachet, an evocative smoky style adored by legions of fans that's every bit as distinctive as its bottles' beige labels and cream wax tops. A product of 'reductive' winemaking, where wines are totally protected from oxygen, it's achieved by pressing slowly for a heavy must full of material, before long barrel ageing on lees. Gone is the hand-to-mouth era when growers lacked the resources to refine their craft. "My grandparents used to have to pick up customers in the centre of the village and drive them to their cellar to try to sell bottles," says Mathis.

Generalising about Côte de Beaune villages is problematic given the numerous terroirs and philosophies in each. If Meursault's 80 domaines make it more diverse than Chassagne, which has around 30, telling them apart in a blind tasting – or from a Puligny, for that matter – isn't easy. But great Montrachet is great Montrachet (Chardonnay's preeminent vineyard, which in 1879 Chassagne and Puligny attached to their names in an act of marketing genius) and difficult to put into words. "This wine has qualities of which neither the Latin nor the French language can explain the sweetness... I am not able to express the delicacy and excellence," wrote Abbé Arnoux in 1728, and I can vouch for English being every bit as futile.

Traditionally Meursault is known for being rich, round Chardonnay with flavours of butter and roasted hazelnuts. Or, as one imbiber had it, ripe peaches picked on a hot day. But if these descriptions fit René Lafon's opulent Meursaults of yore, made with long oak ageing, Jean-Marc Roulot's chiselled versions have more of the 'steely backbone' typically used to portray Puligny wines. So, what to think? "Perhaps there's less wine and more tension in Puligny, and less tension but more wine in Chassagne," says Mathis. Painting broad brushstrokes on butterfly wings is hard.

One thing's for sure, though: there's a camaraderie between the different generations of *vignerons* in Chassagne village. Many, such as Mathis and Clément Colin, and Théo Dancer of Domaine Vincent Dancer, have been schooled in sustainable farming and winemaking by parents who'll soon retire. "Our mums and dads worked hard for years creating everything, and we all have a responsibility to continue in the right way," says the forward-thinking Dancer, who spent two years at Provence's benchmark Domaine de Trévallon learning how it's adapting to climate change. But others, such as Simon Colin (Burgundy has more Colins than an Essex school disco), couldn't have ideas more different to their parents who, having grown up during a less prosperous era with a more marginal growing climate, can be less inclined to see the benefits of regenerative farming. Indeed, when Simon's dad Philippe Colin asked him to join the family domaine, he agreed only on the proviso that they divided the land holdings between them.

At nearby Domaine Paul Pillot, mid-forties Thierry Pillot remembers his own father not being able to understand why he wanted to convert their vineyards to organics, or make other progressive changes, when he took over in 2007. "It was four years before I felt that I'd arrived at an identity for the wines, whereas Chassagne's young new generation know what they want much quicker," says Thierry. While two-thirds of his vines are Chardonnay, he's keen for more Pinot Noir, having planted 0.5ha in Premier Cru 'Clos St Jean', a terroir historically lauded for perfumed reds with a hint of caramel. Many locals still believe that their soils lend themselves better to making reds than whites, especially given many are a mix of Bathonian limestone and clay similar to parts of the Côte de Nuits.

From the start of Appellation d'Origine Contrôlée in the mid-1930s up until the 1950s, two-thirds of Chassagne was red, with Premier Crus 'Clos St Jean' and 'Les Morgeots' fetching similar prices to some Grands Crus further north. Today, Chardonnay conversely makes up over two-thirds of vineyards and, with numerous world-famous *cuvées*, that's unlikely to change. At its best, Chassagne-Montrachet blanc is in a whole other stratosphere compared to rouge. But if frosts continue decimating low-lying limestone and clay village vineyards, growers might consider replanting them with better-suited Pinot. Besides, *vignerons* here are changing perceptions with much-improved reds.

The most impressive Chassagne red that I've drunk is 1978 Bernard Moreau Premier Cru 'Morgeot La Cardeuse', which had a gorgeous roasted scent and no jagged edges. Over the past few years brothers Alex and Benoît Moreau, who had worked together at Domaine Bernard Moreau for 22 vintages, have divided the family vineyards with Benoît establishing his own domaine. Having made his debut 2020s with grapes from friends, he now hones Chassagnes from his own vines, including lovely reds. Avoiding the rustic tannins that can blight Pinot here, he uses light infusions to produce bright, delicate wines with slender cheekbones.

Benoît has spent his life working in Chassagne's vineyards, practising biodynamics and cutting-edge farming methods such as tressage. Redefining his terroirs by separating blocks within some crus into new *cuvées*, and putting his wines through a minimum of two winters in oak, they are already distinctive. 'Les Charrières' 2021, a new village *cuvée* from 50-year-old vines under Grand Cru Criots-Bâtard-Montrachet,

is a gourmand beauty with lots of chew. "It's easy to make a high-acid wine — you pick early," says Benoît. "But it's much harder to make a mineral wine with texture, which is what I'm looking for." From a tiny 0.15ha plot of Chardonnay surrounded by Pinot Noir near the derelict Abbaye de Morgeot, 2021 'La Cardeuse' blanc is a stony-fresh wine of Grand Cru proportions with a hint of white chocolate — a flavour that I can't get enough of in top white Burgundy.

A similar balance between gourmand pâtisserie and mineral tension is what makes mature vintages of Domaine Ramonet — Chassagne's most renowned estate — so alluring. Likewise, a few doors down at Domaine Lamy-Caillat, where husband and wife Florence Lamy and Sébastien Caillat are producing some of my favourite Côte de Beaune whites. Sébastien works at Florence's family's Domaine Lamy-Pillot during the day, but in 2008 the couple rented 1.2ha of vines to make their own whites with a more uncompromising approach. Releasing 500 cases a year from top Premiers Crus such as 'Les Caillerets' — a vineyard that was planted entirely with Pinot Noir during the Second World War — they make dense-textured old-school classics built for the long haul.

Sébastien, a modest elder statesman of the village in his late forties, trained as an engineer, so it's not just the wine here that's bespoke. He made his cellar's tasting table displaying their vineyard soils with matching metal stools, and restored a 1960s Vaslin press, gleaming like a factory-fresh *USS Enterprise* in the winery. Decades ago, the Vaslin was ubiquitous in Burgundy, slowly pressing heavy musts, as opposed to the thinner, more brittle juice from modern pneumatic presses (believed to be a cause of the premature oxidation that blighted many whites from the mid-'90s on). Add to this meticulous farming and a particularly damp, cold and stable cellar — which Sébastien says is as much a part of their terroir as the soils, vines, pruning, harvesting and barrels — and you have a snapshot of Lamy-Caillat's formula for success. "We do everything carefully by hand, but the attention we get because of the wines is crazy — a bit like the world today," says Sébastien. Chassagne's coming generation had better get ready for a new legion of admirers. ●

A SHORTCUT TO DRINKING GREAT WHITE BURGUNDY

THE BURGUNDIAN EFFECT
COTE D'OR INFLUENCE ON GREAT EUROPEAN WINES

Domaine Paul Pillot
Bourgogne Blanc
$$$

Domaine Roulot
Bourgogne Blanc
$$$$

Domaine Ramonet
St-Aubin Premier Cru
'Les Murgers des Dents de Chien'
$$$$

Domaine Leflaive
Puligny-Montrachet Premier Cru
'Les Pucelles'
$$$$

Domaine Benoît Moreau
Bâtard-Montrachet
$$$$-$$$$$

Emidio Pepe
Abruzzo, Italy
$$$-$$$$

In the late 1960s Emidio Pepe escaped his family's stock-in-trade as poor agricultural workers by creating an international market for his Abruzzo wines, flying to New York City with four bottles in a suitcase, and touring Italian restaurants around Europe to sell them from the boot of his car. Over half a century on, his traditionalist (and often idiosyncratic) methods are being sympathetically refined by his granddaughter, Chiara Pepe. Having spent time learning winemaking at Dijon University, with several days a week working at Savigny-lès-Beaune's Chandon de Briailles and tasting at other leading domaines, in 2020 she returned to Abruzzo to take over the estate with a focus on improving the quality of its work in the vineyards and taking steps toward greater precision in its Montepulciano d'Abruzzo and Trebbiano d'Abruzzo (there's now a sorting table in the winery for the first time). Emidio's very unusual process for releasing old vintages — where bottles were uncorked and decanted into new ones — has even been curtailed, although drinkers who venerate the domaine's soulful-rustic-country style shouldn't worry about the wines being unnecessarily cleaned up. 2021 Emidio Pepe Cerasuolo d'Abruzzo has a depth and vitality far beyond its humble designation.

Dominio del Águila
'Viñas Viejas'
Ribera del Duero, Spain
$$$

Dalamára
Xinomavro
Naoussa, Greece
$$$

When Dominio del Águila's Jorge Monzón says he learnt that "Grands Crus can be found in many places" from two years working at Domaine de la Romanée-Conti, you know he's not lacking aspirations. Producing elegant Ribera del Duero reds from old vineyards, he also makes the rare 'Viñas Viejas' Albillo Mayor (from 100 year+ old vines grown at 800m, trodden by foot, then aged in French oak for over two and a half years), one of the most intriguing whites to emerge from Spain in years. The first thing that strikes you about 2019 'Viñas Viejas' is its refined Burgundy-esque nose, a harmonious blend of citrus and expensive oak. It tells you it's made by an ambitious grower. The wine has a full texture, from a combination of terroir and extended ageing, and a refreshing salinity. But Albillo Mayor's low acidity sets it apart from Chardonnay. The 2018, on the other hand, is a different beast. On first whiff, some experienced tasters have confused its gunflinty fragrance with Meursault's Jean-François Coche at the height of his powers. It's obvious from where Jorge Monzón is drawing creative inspiration for his ground-breaking wines.

Just like Spain, the improvements in Greek winemaking over the past decade have been remarkable. Where previously commercial wineries farming bland 'international' grapes, or badly educated winemakers extracting huge amounts of tannins from formidably tannic grapes dominated, the emergence of vignerons such as Santorini's Haridimos Hatzidakis, Crete's Gianni Economou, and Naoussa's Kostis Dalamáras proved the nation was capable of world-class wines. Dalamáras studied oenology in France before taking a job at Domaine Trapet in Gevrey-Chambertin, among others, where he learnt to hone in on finesse rather than power, oak and alcohol — a skill he has since applied to his homeland's Xinomavro grape. Dalamára produces some of northern Greece's most age-worthy reds, full of sunshine, herbs and black olives. You must try them.

13

SCHOOL OF ROCK

Reinventing Muscadet, Loire Valley, France

Muscadet vines,
Loire Valley,
France.

It all comes back to Burgundy, as so many things about wine do. Or, more specifically, to the fact that great bottles are made through the miraculous amalgamation of climate, soil and human philosophy known as 'terroir'. Yet when the familiar feeling hits, I'm not in eastern France but a ramshackle outbuilding-cum-tasting room in Muscadet, south-east of Nantes on the Atlantic coast. A moment of clarity as enlightening as tasting different crus in a Vosne-Romanée cellar for the first time; a shock at the profound variations in taste of a single grape variety grown on neighbouring soils, just feet away from one another.

Rémi Branger, a *vigneron* with a thick black beard and piercing brown eyes at the helm of Domaine de la Pépière, serves me four wines made in four of Muscadet's ten recently defined Crus Communaux: 'Clisson', 'Gorges', 'Monnières-St Fiacre' and 'Château-Thébaud'. One grape, one hand, across different subzones – a wide range of flavours. I hadn't expected to find such character and precision in Muscadet, one of the great also-rans of French regions. Made from Melon de Bourgogne (now comically rechristened as 'Melon B' by authorities), the wine has long been thought of as a cheap, innocuous, moderate-alcohol accompaniment for seafood, lacking the sophistication or longevity of noble Chardonnay or Chenin Blanc. But Muscadet has been quietly improving and Pépière, having started producing its first single-vineyard *cuvée* 'Clos des Briords' at the turn of the millennium, is at the vanguard of its bid to be recast as a serious wine of place. Linear and intense, with a salty finish comparable to Chablis, stony 'Clisson' (from gravel and pebble soils) offers a revelatory contrast to the subtly herbaceous, smoky 'Gorges' (a mix of quartz, gabbros and clay).

That Muscadet's cru classification now exists is due to the work of Pépière and contemporaries such as domaines Luneau-Papin and La Louvetrie. If for decades it was enough for Muscadet to be one of far fewer cheap white wines, with producers using industrial farming to harvest high yields and make big quantities of low-quality wines, the growth in popularity of everything from Kiwi Sauvignon Blanc to Italian Pinot Grigio meant its survival was far from assured. Realising that Muscadet must evolve in order to prosper, a handful of these domaines undertook extensive soil studies and mapping, pushing for improvements in organic farming and winemaking.

"My model is Burgundy," the grand-moustachioed Jo Landron of Domaine de la Louvetrie, who made his debut benchmark single-vineyard 'Le Fief du Breil' in 1982, tells me. "At its best Muscadet illustrates what's great about French winemaking — *vignerons* taking care of the soil and finding differences between the terroirs. When you have only one grape you can really see the variety of taste." As he hands me different rocks made of orthogneiss, granite and limestone to illustrate his vineyards' soils, there's no doubting Landron's message: Cru Muscadet is a serious terroir wine.

Other Muscadet producers have named their wines after the soil in which they were grown, such as 'Expression de Gneiss' and 'Orthogneiss' at Guy Bossard's ground-breaking Domaine de L'Ecu. Now owned by Fred Niger, whose winery is complete with many amphorae and a crystal cellar, it represents the more experimental side of modern wine. But it's not uncommon to spot amphorae, concrete eggs, or fashionable Stockinger oak fermentation vessels in Muscadet domaines — all of which traditionally have no place in its production — a sign of the collective ambition to elevate the wines. In fact, most estates here don't have actual cellars, but ground-floor wineries with large glass-lined concrete tanks sunk into the floors, where wines lie inert, free from intervention for many months.

The time they spend there on their 'lees' (dead yeast cells) develops their body and structure, although if left too long they become flabby and uninteresting. In 1977 Muscadet introduced the term 'sur lie' as a way of distinguishing quality, although today it only guarantees that a wine was bottled the year after harvest, with many high-quality, longer-aged *cuvées* falling outside the designation.

After a lot of tasting, I'm convinced that Muscadet needs to be as pure as possible to be at its best. If oak ageing benefits white Burgundy by allowing an interchange of oxygen and, in small doses, providing a complementary flavour, with Melon de Bourgogne it often obtrudes like cheap plastic surgery. For me, the best wines are full of energy and saline minerality as a result of their terroir.

"The identity of Muscadet is unique," says Pierre-Marie Luneau of Domaine Luneau-Papin, located in Le Landreau. "We don't have the complexity of Burgundy, or the aromatics of Sauvignon Blanc, but we have saltiness and moderate alcohol." Luneau is spot on: with today's zeitgeist venerating freshness and restraint his wines have become some of our restaurants' bestsellers, buoyed up by their exceptional affordability.

Certainly, it's hard to think of many classic whites that offer as good a flavour-to-price ratio as Luneau-Papin's 'Le L d'Or', and the early vintages of Jean-Baptiste Hardy, one of the region's newest producers. Leaving his family estates in Mouzillon-Tillières (one of the ten recently defined Crus

Jo Landron, Domaine de la Louvetrie, La Haie-Fouassière, Muscadet.

Pierre-Marie
Luneau, Domaine
Luneau-Papin,
Le Landreau,
Muscadet.

Communaux) to work with Jean-Marc Roulot — one of Meursault's best
vignerons — he returned in 2018 and applied many of the ideas he'd learnt.
Perhaps just as Cru Beaujolais has become increasingly coveted by red
Burgundy lovers who haven't been able to keep up with rising tariffs, so
Cru Muscadet might increasingly appeal to those priced out of many of the
top whites. When I ask Pierre-Marie Luneau if he thinks his wines have
the capacity to improve with bottle age he disappears into his stockroom
and returns a few minutes later with a 2003 'Le L d'Or' that is a ringer for
a rich, mature Chablis. From industrial also-ran to artisanal contender,
Cru Muscadet's time has come. ●

A SHORTCUT TO DRINKING GREAT MUSCADET

MY FAVOURITE 'MINERAL' WHITE WINE, CHABLIS, NORTHERN BURGUNDY, FRANCE

Domaine Luneau-Papin
Muscadet 'Le L d'Or'
$$

Jean-Baptiste Hardy
Muscadet 'Fief de Chaintre'
$$$

Domaine de la Pépière
Muscadet 'Clisson'
$$$

Domaine de Bellevue
Muscadet, Granite 'Clos des Perrières'
$$$

Domaine de la Louvetrie
Muscadet 'Le Fief du Breil'
$$

If 'salinity' is one of wine's most overused descriptors, then 'minerality' has long been one of its most derided. Many people HATE it, considering it bad science. But for me, 'minerality', used with artistic licence, is handy shorthand for aromas and flavours such as salt/smoke/stone as opposed to those in a fruit/flower register. Rub a couple of rocks together under your nose and you'll get what I mean. Similarly, wine merchant Maurice Healy suggested the word 'fumosity' for such impressions in his book Stay Me with Flagons (1940): "Fumosity is a word that seeks ancient lineage; but I use it, here and elsewhere, as depicting a particular bouquet and flavour that suggests that the vintagers have ground flints into the must." Nothing describes the sensation of drinking the wines of Chablis in northern Burgundy so well.

Few whites are as distinguished as top Chablis, with domaines Raveneau and Dauvissat having both long made compelling arguments to be among the greatest winemakers in France. Close by in the village a younger generation is hot on their heels, focusing on regenerative farming and producing cuvées with similarly seaweedy, briny, earthy, often honeyed/lactic dairy flavours. Domaines such as Eleni and Édouard Vocoret who, having refined their craft on village vineyards and one Premier Cru, find their estate magnified by the addition of the appellation's best crus courtesy of Édouard's family. Or Domaine Pattes Loup, where perfectionist Thomas Pico plants trees and radishes between rows of biodynamic vines to give nitrogen to the soil, turning carbon from the air into life-supporting oxygen (the widespread toxic fertiliser diammonium phosphate (DAP) does a similar job but to the detriment of the environment). Pico's Chablis is aged for a minimum of two-and-a-half years to develop texture with minimal added sulphur, honing in on small details to make his dream wines.

Domaine Eleni & Édouard Vocoret
Chablis 'Le Bas de Chapelot'
$$$

Domaine Pattes Loup
Chablis Premier Cru 'Beauregard'
$$$

Domaine Alice & Olivier de Moor
Chablis 'L'Humeur du Temps'
$$$

Vincent Dauvissat
Chablis Grand Cru 'Les Preuses'
$$$$

Domaine Raveneau
Chablis Grand Cru 'Les Clos'
$$$$$

Thomas Pico, Domaine Pattes Loup, Chablis.

14

CHIANTI (NOT CHIANTI)

*Mastering the
sensual side of Sangiovese in
Tuscany, Italy*

Radda in Chianti,
Tuscany, Italy.

Italian wine is complicated. Never mind the Côte d'Or, whose intricacies are often seen as wine culture's most insurmountable cliff-face, the Bel Paese's wine landscape—daunting numbers of unusual grape varieties and vehement local differences of opinion—has left me scratching my head far more frequently. Growing up in pre-internet England, few things could sound as impenetrable as 'Refosco dal Peduncolo Rosso' or 'Ribolla Gialla', especially compared to the ubiquitous Chardonnay. But the more I explore Italy, the more enamoured I become with the sensual side of its most-planted and routinely abused red grape—Sangiovese—discovering how, in its Tuscan heartlands, it reaches heights I presumed were only offered by Burgundian Pinot Noir.

Delicate, floral, exotic; there are stylistic similarities between A-grade Vosne-Romanée and Brunello di Montalcino, the most obvious difference being an extra sweetness to fruit born of Mediterranean sunbeams rather than Côte de Nuits mists. In the hands of the late Burgundian *vigneron* Henri Jayer, or Tuscan master-taster Giulio Gambelli (an influential advocate of single-variety *cuvées*, who worked as a consultant for a roll call of leading estates), both Pinot Noir and Sangiovese combine opulent restraint with electrifying energy. And just as those wizards were able to put two and two together and come up with a million, a new wave of wine-makers, inspired by their often twice- or thrice-removed influences, are pulling off the same magic in up-and-coming appellations.

Radda, a sub-region of Tuscany's Chianti Classico DOCG, is somewhere that has literally found its place in the sun. A high-altitude landscape of hills, forests, olive groves and cypress trees, where only 10% is under vine, Radda is remarkable both for the number of its *vignerons* organically farming a pure, finessed style of Sangiovese, and for how climate change has improved ripening of its cool vineyards. For decades, Radda lived in the shadow of its celebrated neighbour, Panzano, whose galestro soils and average 50m lower elevation produce riper, darker, full-bodied Chianti. But in recent years their relationship has evolved. That's not to say that Panzano's big names such as Fontodi – an early adopter of organics and, with its 'Flaccianello' *cuvée*, producer of one of the first 100% Sangioveses to be acclaimed on the world stage – are not still important. It's just that, where once Radda wines were considered too lean, acidic and out of kilter with the trend for modern 'Parker' styles, the zeitgeist has swung in its favour. One *vigneron* tells me: "We're lucky to be in Radda."

Of course, many drinkers still venerate showy, high-alcohol wines, but for me Sangiovese is best when handled gently, using traditional techniques to produce lighter colours with fine powdery tannins and Pinot-esque strawberry/cherry fruit. The best Radda wines are imbued with freshness and stone-like minerality, with typical aromas of violets, undergrowth, mushrooms and – with age – blood. Although historically the climate here made it hard to ripen tricky Sangiovese, accomplished estates have long had the know-how. One of my favourites is Montevertine, producer of iconic 100% Sangiovese 'Le Pergole Torte', a wine that was created by the iconoclastic Sergio Manetti, with consultant Giulio Gambelli.

Italy today is dominated by wine consultants, employed to produce proficient but often lifeless wines by estate owners who have made their fortunes in other industries. While the majority are incentivised to prioritise consistency over character, Gambelli, who died in 2012, was a man of a different class and time. Back in 1967, when he encouraged his childhood friend Manetti, a wine and art lover who owned a metal manufacturing business in nearby Poggibonsi, to buy Montevertine, he provided the winemaking suss to propel the estate to renown. Nicknamed Bicchierino, or 'Little Glass', Gambelli had learnt his craft as assistant to Tancredi Biondi Santi of Brunello di Montalcino's founding family, under whose tutelage he became a *maestro assaggiatore* ('master taster') so venerated that winery chemists were said to have calibrated their instruments to his palate. Like his mentor, he believed Sangiovese was at its best as a mono-variety wine, rather than blended with international grapes, and went on to consult for several now benchmark estates, including Montalcino's Soldera. So profound was his influence that some use the adjective *'gambelliano'* to denote true Sangiovese.

Manetti and Gambelli made the debut Montevertine Chianti Classico in 1971, which by law at the time had to include the white grapes Malvasia and Trebbiano, as well as Sangiovese, Canaiolo and Colorino. Unconvinced of the value of adding whites – which others used to soften and bulk out wine – to the blend, the duo decided to flout the DOCG laws and make the wine they dreamed of with pure Sangiovese, beginning their experiments in 1975. Two years later they filled five oak *barriques* bought from Burgundy's Domaine de la Romanée-Conti with the first-ever 100% Sangiovese commercially produced in the area, christened 'Le Pergole Torte' ('The Twisted Pergolas') after one of Montevertine's founding vineyards.

Although today the fruit for 'Le Pergole Torte' comes from old vines scattered around the Montevertine estate, it is still made using the same old-school methods. Sold as a Vino da Tavola (now IGT) outside Chianti Classico DOCG, 'Le Pergole Torte' quickly achieved impressive results; so much so that in 1981 Manetti offered it to the Consorzio Vino Chianti Classico for consideration as a Chianti Classico Riserva, a premium wine that would help bolster the DOCG's reputation. "Not suitable for bottling" was its response. Exasperated, Manetti also withdrew Montevertine from the appellation, and began releasing all of his wines as Vino da Tavola.

Leaving Chianti Classico was a masterstroke. Unlike Burgundy, where terroir is sacrosanct and domaines print vineyard names in big fonts and their own names much smaller on their labels, Chianti producers' reputations can be stifled by the DOCG's ambiguous values. Radda in the '80s was the right time and place to present drinkers with something revolutionary — a Chianti Classico that wasn't a Chianti Classico — and before long the outstanding 1985 vintage sent Montevertine's reputation into the stratosphere. Drinking 1985 'Le Pergole Torte', some four decades on from harvest, was a remarkable experience. As expected, its nose was evolved with exotic spices and dried blood, but I was surprised by the palate's extraordinary youth and richness, with the lively acidity that is Radda's hallmark. Likewise, 2007 'Le Pergole Torte' was almost enough to render me speechless. With its perfume of truffles, damp soil, raspberry lozenges, balsamic vinegar and sunshine, it is the kind of Italian wine that makes me pine for an old country I don't have any business pining for.

Today both Gambelli and Manetti are long gone, but their spirit remains through Manetti's son Martino. Visiting Montevertine at the beginning of October I was surprised to find Martino outside his winery, sorting through the last of the harvest — small, plump pellets of Sangiovese easily mistaken for blueberries. Given Burgundy finished picking five weeks earlier, it is telling how much hang-time Radda's altitude demands. "Sangiovese can make a very elegant wine or a very raw wine," says Martino. "But to be elegant it needs ripeness from a late harvest. I'm not interested in wines with massive body, structure, colour and alcohol — for me a great wine is finessed and persistent."

Beside 'Le Pergole Torte' — whose labels were painted by artist Alberto Manfredi, adding a distinct identity to one of Italy's most cult Sangioveses — Manetti makes the entry-level 'Pian del Ciampolo', and eponymous 'Montevertine', both blends of Sangiovese, Canaiolo and Colorino, the latter his equivalent of Chianti Classico. For me, 'Montevertine' is one of the best-value fine wines anywhere in the world, with a grace and longevity that can rival its exalted sibling at a fraction of the price.

But if Montevertine is a long-established beacon of authenticity in oceans of industrially made Italian wines, what's so exciting about Radda's future is embodied by Vignaioli di Radda, an association of 24 local growers, nearly all certified organic, of which Manetti is vice president. "I'm part of a new generation here that exchanges ideas, experiences and information," says Manetti's friend, and president of the association, Roberto Bianchi. Including leading estates such as Monteraponi and Poggerino — both of whose harmonious wines have become 'buy-on-sight' selections for me — growers meet up every month to taste and support one another's work. "Before, it wasn't conceivable to do this — it would've just been people saying 'My wine is the only drinkable wine on earth!'" says Bianchi, laughing.

If such inclusivity, coupled with rising temperatures, really does mean that Radda has found its place in the sun, then Bianchi's Val delle Corti estate might be said to have metaphorically moved on to a lounger by the pool. Indeed, because all Bianchi's vineyards are planted on east-facing slopes, and are thus especially cool even for Radda, his estate has gained more than most. In the 1990s, Val delle Corti fruit would often struggle to mature, producing astringent wines, but now makes consistently ripe and direct Chianti Classico. Having swiftly left his first career as a teacher to take over the family estate when his father Giorgio died in 1999, he acknowledges his Vignaioli di Radda comrades as the guiding force behind his success. Especially Sean O'Callaghan of Tenuta di Carleone.

If anyone could be described as *gambelliano*, it is Sean O'Callaghan, the self-styled Il Guercio ('One-eyed Rascal'). An affable Englishman with, you guessed it, one working eye, O'Callaghan first came on holiday to Chianti in 1989, hoping to learn about wine, and began working for John Dunkley, another expat, at Riecine two years later. Three decades on, Sean is at the forefront of Radda's renaissance, crafting exceptionally pure Sangiovese as head winemaker at Tenuta di Carleone since its debut vintage in 2015. "I'm trying to make the 'Pergole Tortes' of the '90s," O'Callaghan tells me. "But with climate change that's difficult. Back then the wines were between 12.5% and 13% alcohol but now we have to work to keep them under 14%."

Pushing macerations for up to two months — as Biondi Santi often did — and including some stems, he treads a fine line between success and failure. These uncompromising methods are a way of developing freshness and flavour while dropping colour, which he feels isn't so

Roberto Bianchi,
Val delle Corti,
Radda in Chianti.

important, but also creates volatile acidity, something most winemakers try to eliminate at all costs. But although too much VA invariably kills wines, in tiny quantities it adds a balsamic-esque prickle of interest to many of the world's most characterful reds, from old-school Barolo to the Cornas of Thierry Allemand in the Northern Rhône. For that matter, Gambelli himself was said to have disliked the modern preoccupation with eradicating it, believing it helped deliver supple, rounder wines. But whatever the techniques, Tenuta di Carleone's future classic 'Uno' is exactly the kind of delicate, floral Sangiovese that energises my love for 'Chianti Not Chianti', and keeps bringing me back for more. "The problem with many people here is they try to make something that's complex and big, and they totally lose the plot," says O'Callaghan. "Sangiovese is something that should be really... clear." ●

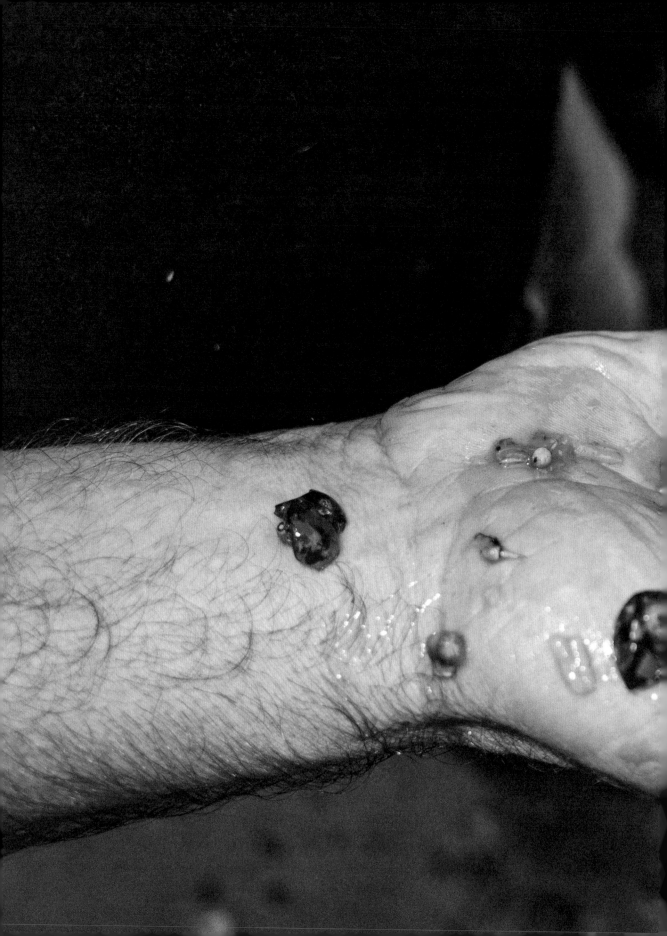

Radda in Chianti is a commune located north of Siena and south-east of Florence in Tuscany.

A SHORTCUT TO DRINKING GREAT CHIANTI (NOT CHIANTI)

Val delle Corti
Chianti Classico Riserva
$$

Poggerino
Chianti Classico
$$

Monteraponi
'Baron' Ugo'
Toscana IGT
$$$

Tenuta di Carleone
'Uno'
Toscana IGT
$$$

Montevertine
'Le Pergole Torte'
Toscana IGT
$$$$

15

IT'S JUST BEGUN, PART TWO

Fresh ideas and energy in Piedmont, north-west Italy

Philine Isabelle
Dienger,
Monforte d'Alba,
Piedmont.

A great mind once said that people don't believe in ideas, they believe in people who believe in ideas. And if any wine region has had more than its share of opinionated believers—convinced that their way is the only way—it's Langhe in north-west Italy. Take Angelo Gaja, Barbaresco's most celebrated son, for example. Seeing that the Bordeaux-centric wine world wouldn't come to his dirt-poor part of Piedmont, he took Piedmont to the world, generating acclaim for his then-exotic Nebbiolos during the '70s. Legion drinkers followed suit. Or Elio Altare, who returned to Barolo from visiting Château Margaux with game-changing ideas about how hygiene would improve local winemaking. Asking Margaux what he should do to make a wine as great as its own, he was told: "clean up".

But not all Piedmontese looked west for inspiration. Old-school master Giuseppe Rinaldi hated the '90s trend for softening Nebbiolo's fierce tannin and concentrating fruit to make it accessible to modern palates. He believed Barolo should be the antithesis of instant gratification, his appreciation for French influence symbolised by a wooden chair in his winery displaying the legend "The best use for *barriques*".

After years of contrasting ideologies that labelled Langhe domaines as either 'modernist' or 'traditionalist', today's winemakers blur generalisations and take the best of both. In Barbaresco, Gaia Gaja inherited the mantle of dynamo-in-chief from Angelo, and is as serious about world domination as her father ever was. Sisters Carlotta and Marta Rinaldi, meanwhile, took over the making of the family's traditional-styled wines several years before their dad Giuseppe died in 2017, albeit with—shock horror—early-drinking pleasure to be found (you don't need to be a masochist to enjoy 2019 Rinaldi Barolo 'Brunate', whose explosive fruit and supple tannins

thrill at an early age). Of course, the typical Piedmontese mindset remains steadfastly no-nonsense and to the point, but rising average growing temperatures and improved farming, winemaking and distribution have transformed Barolo and Barbaresco from impoverished Italian obscurities lacking Cru Classé-style appeal to regular fixtures on thrill-seeking dining tables. And besides the changing of the guard at now-celebrated domaines, there is also an influx of determined immigrants bringing new energy to the Langhe.

You've got to have strong beliefs to set out to make Barolo from nowhere. In fact, you've got to have nuts of steel to stand on the precipice of the great rural unknown and launch yourself in, considering the sweat it demands with no guarantee of success. Years ago, when local *vignerons* were hard up, it would've been unthinkable for an outsider to want to do it. Piedmont, unlike Burgundy, to which it is often compared due to its intricate map of terroirs, has no track record for attracting talented foreign *vignerons* such as Ted Lemon, erstwhile American cellar master at Meursault's Domaine Roulot, or the late Californian trailblazer Jim Clendenen. Not only are there huge set-up costs – €25,000 per traditional oak *botte* soon adds up – but often a language barrier too.

"I remember thinking: I've no idea what I'm signing away," American winemaker Alan Manley tells me of the day he registered his Monforte d'Alba winery, Margherita Otto, with the Piedmontese authorities. Besides, making Barolo is a long game. You see the words 'Nebbiolo atta a Barolo' – 'destined to become Barolo' – writ in large letters on *botti* across the appellation, as Nebbiolo can't legally be classified as Barolo before 38 months of ageing, 18 of which must be in wood cask. And if you've planted your own vineyards, you've got to wait seven years for their fruit to be eligible for inclusion.

Fortunately for fledgling winemakers, Barolo is not the only appellation in Piedmont. Compared to wine regions such as Bordeaux or the Côte d'Or, Piedmont has a more diverse polyculture of crops and woodland, with the pre-eminent Nebbiolo – a fickle, site-sensitive grape that is first to bud and last to ripen – making up 9% of vineyards. A variety of international and off-trend native grapes abounds, with many of the best new winemakers producing supple, high-acid Barberas, tannic Dolcettos (a grape that was as highly valued as Nebbiolo during the '60s), as well as less prestigious Langhe Nebbiolo wines – a DOC in which Nebbiolo from Barolo, Barbaresco and Roero may be declassified – to build reputations while Barolos and Barbarescos age.

Besides chutzpah and a burning desire to express a sense of place and vintage, what do Piedmont's new believers share? Their forebears were first to lower yields, reintroduce organic farming and improve cellar cleanliness and storage, immeasurably benefiting consistency (I've opened far more faulty old Italian wines than French over the years), but structured Nebbiolo is an acquired taste that still requires explaining. Although traditionally Barolo is made from a blend of vineyards, balancing out both under- and over-ripe fruit, fledgling estates don't have the land to do this, even if they want to. Besides, vinifying single-vineyard crus à la Burgundy is very much in vogue. One thing's for sure, though: to love Barolo and Barbaresco, whose countless microclimates and sensibilities often make them impossible to tell apart, you've got to love firm tannins and lively acidity as much as their dramatic rose petal and tar perfumes.

Lalù's Luisa
Sala and Lara
Rocchetti with
Moka and Orsa,
Serralunga
d'Alba.

"Nebbiolo has amazing qualities but generosity isn't always one of them," says Tom Myers, a single-minded Kiwi who used a crowdfunding campaign to sell future allocations of his own Barolos to set up his domaine – Cantina D'Arcy – in 2020. "My favourite ever wines, from Domaine Leroy and Soldera, are all immediately generous and intellectually stimulating – so I asked myself what I had to do with Nebbiolo to get that kind of experience." A taste of his gorgeous debut 2020 Barolo 'Preda', which contained 50% whole bunches in the fermentation adding a smoky-spiciness to sumptuous sweet fruit, shows that such grand aspirations are far from talk.

Myers and his friend Philine Isabelle Dienger are making two different expressions of Barolo's 'Preda' vineyard that will be fascinating to follow over coming years. Having separately learnt their craft from Alto Adige to Volnay ("The cool thing about having worked in different places is that you've many different ideas about wine", says Myers), the pair met via mutual friends at Rinaldi and, with the help of the sisters, signed a short-term lease on the 1.2ha Nebbiolo-planted vineyard 'Preda', dividing the vines between them and establishing their own estates (D'Arcy is Myers' grandmother's maiden name; Dienger drops her surname for 'Philine Isabelle').

Visiting Dienger – a young German with an infectious charm – in her Monforte cellar, I was wowed by the almost Vosne-Romanée-esque nobility of her 2020 Barolo 'Preda', an elegant red with very fine sandy tannins. Citing Japanese craftsmanship as an influence – notably the idea that masterworks are made up of countless seemingly inconsequential tiny decisions – she uses biodynamics and progressive farming techniques such as tressage, where vines are woven into arches rather than cut, to aid ripening and protect the plants from stress that might otherwise manifest as harsh tannins.

Just as D'Arcy and Philine Isabelle were helped to life by Rinaldi, so Margherita Otto comes from an esteemed traditionalist pedigree – winemaker Alan Manley has worked at the side of Maria Teresa Mascarello for 11 years. An ex-Colorado restaurateur, Manley gained experience in the cellars of several celebrated Piedmontese domaines before moving permanently to Italy and vinifying his debut 2015 vintage in the Mascarello winery. Again, I was taken aback by such accomplished wines: fleshy without heaviness and genuinely complex, with perfumes that are very difficult to explain.

Drinking interstellar vino is essential for understanding what's achievable when making it, and many of this coming generation take inspiration from Burgundy. Some, like Giulia Negri, who left home in Milan to take over her family's old estate high up on Barolo's Serradenari mountain, make regular pilgrimages to top *vignerons* such as Pierre-Yves Colin-Morey in Chassagne-Montrachet to learn, while Torinese college friends Luisa Sala and Lara Rocchetti spent harvests at Comtes Lafon and Cécile Tremblay while training at La Morra's benchmark Trediberri, prior to starting Lalù in 2019. "Settling in the countryside as city girl outsiders was challenging," says Sala, citing the support of Piedmont's expat community as essential to their success. If one of the hallmarks of a 'fine' wine is that it expresses something about where it's grown, these newcomers, unencumbered by blood politics, say it by following their own ideas. "Great Barolo is just like the people – hard and straight," Lara tells me. Once you've acquired the taste, there's no turning back. ●

Trediberri
Barolo 'Berri'
$$$

Cà di Press
Barolo del Comune di Monforte d'Alba
$$$

Cantina D'Arcy
Barolo 'Preda'
$$$$

Philine Isabelle
Barolo 'Preda'
$$$$

Bartolo Mascarello
Barolo
$$$$

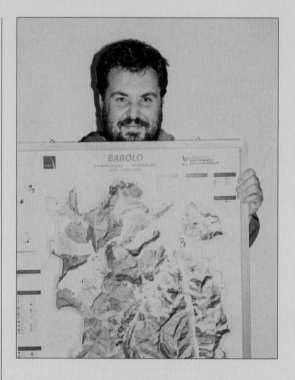

Trediberri's Nicola Oberto exemplifies the best of Barolo's new old-school winemakers.

PIEDMONTESE MASTERS
SURE BETS FOR SUPERLATIVE LANGHE DRINKING

Piero Busso
Barbaresco
$$-$$$

Barbaresco has more famous wines, but none I'd rather drink than Piero Busso. That Busso's wines are not more famous is puzzling, but represents an opportunity for those who love to drink world-class vino without paying hundreds of pounds. Founded in the 1950s by Guido Busso, the winery is now headed by his grandson Pierguido 'Pier' Busso — a thoughtful, deftly skilled vigneron who knows exactly the kind of wine he wants to make. "Travelling and tasting wine was the best schooling I had," says Pier, next to scores of empty bottles from other top European domaines in his winery. "Nebbiolo is not an easy wine, so I try to make one that gently reflects where it's grown." Indeed, Busso's four Barbaresco crus are tender yet expansive. His roster of single-vineyard crus begins with 'Mondino', typically the most open early in life with the softest tannins; then 'Albesani', a floral wine that combines austerity and elegance; 'Gallina', which sits at the same altitude as 'Albesani', more powerful with sweet tannins; and 'San Stunet', his highest-altitude vineyard and richest Barbaresco that retains lots of freshness in warmer vintages.

Giuseppe Rinaldi
Barolo
$$$$

"I love tannins and the austere side of Barolo — I don't want to make wines that're just easy to drink," says Carlotta Rinaldi, who, along with her sister Marta, runs the Giuseppe Rinaldi estate in Barolo town. Like their larger-than-life vet-cum-vigneron father who railed against the use of international grapes and barriques in his hometown, his daughters don't venerate accessibility as the most essential characteristic of wine. They'd much rather make something that demands thought on the part of the drinker. Even if the style of their more recent vintages — buoyed by rising temperatures fully ripening their crops every year — doesn't necessitate the extended cellar ageing of their father's to make beautiful drinking. The sisters recently bought vines in Barolo's 'Bussia' cru, softening their stance on bottling a new, gloriously rich single-vineyard cru (the Barolo tradition of blending vineyards is rooted in an era when many struggled for maturity). For me, wines such as 2006 and 2019 'Brunate-Le Coste' represent the best of Barolo — monsters with a delicate touch.

THERE MAY BE TRUFFLE AHEAD

16

*Truffles' fragrances can be
as compelling as the
finest of wines*

Besides grouse and shellfish, truffles are my favourite foods to serve with very special bottles of wine, although many drinkers are apprehensive about these enigmatic delicacies. Perhaps they feel that they are catnip for the affected like caviar or Wagyu beef — ingredients that are only luxurious because they're perceived to be so by a wealthy demographic with cash to burn. But while they're undoubtedly expensive, prized for their heady perfumes and the theatrical ritual of serving, truffles have the power to induce delirium like a great Barolo or Burgundy, whose fragrances they echo. The last time I put price out of mind and succumbed to the lure of a white truffle, my kitchen filled with exotic aroma clouds that blended with the fragrance of René Engel Échézeaux in a way that can only be described as miraculous. But before getting carried away with quasi-religious talk, we should first ask a simple question: what is a truffle anyway?

A truffle is a strong-smelling fungus that looks a bit like a scaly potato that grows near the roots of different tree species that, along with climatic and soil variations, exert as much influence over flavour characteristics as terroir does on wine grapes. There are over 40 varieties, including the common, mushroom-like summer and autumn truffle, but the two that really quicken the pulse of enlightened imbibers are the Périgord black (*Tuber melanosporum*), prized by the French, and the Piedmont white (*Tuber magnatum*), which the Italians consider superior — of course. Both are seasonal, the white appearing between September and January, and the black from December through February. For most of the year a truffle grows underground, drawing sugars from tree roots and nutrients from the soil, but in order to proliferate, it needs an animal to dig it up, eat it, then disperse its spores in its faeces (circle of life, innit). It does this by secreting pungent pheromones irresistibly drawing animals and humans towards it.

Pigs were once customary for truffle hunting but their tendency to snaffle specimens and draw attention to secret locations make dogs de rigueur today. Truffle hunting is a big business with an unsavoury underbelly – low-quality truffles are embellished to look more expensive, and gangs use any means necessary to stay ahead. "One of the dark sides of the white truffle season is the lengths some hunters will go to in order to protect their patch," says *vigneronne* Carlotta Rinaldi. "My father Giuseppe was first a vet and I remember as a kid the number of dogs he saved from poisoning in autumn, often performing last-minute surgeries on the cellar floor. Thankfully that doesn't happen as often any more." Indeed, truffle hunting is a deadly serious métier, and not necessarily passed on to future generations. In the excellent feature documentary *The Truffle Hunters* (2020), a man remonstrates with an elder to divulge the whereabouts of his hunting grounds before he dies. "But if you had a child you'd show them!" the man pleads. "NEVER!" replies the elder.

This highly competitive culture – and the fact that hunters can cover unforgiving terrain for many hours without reward – is what makes truffles so expensive. In November 2023, Wiltshire Truffles, one of Noble Rot restaurants' suppliers, was selling first-class white truffles for £3,200 a kilo, making a 100g nugget, shaved over tagliolini for four jolly imbibers, cost £320 wholesale (which at UK retail prices would be double). Is it worth it? A good truffle can undoubtedly be the centrepiece of a very exhilarating dinner. Mind-boggling, too, to imagine the man-hours that go into finding the 30–40kg of truffles a week that the company supplies to chefs at the height of the season.

"When Italians say that white truffles from other countries are no good, it's just not true," says Wiltshire Truffles' Zak Frost, who sells truffles from around the world. "I'd guess less than 5% of truffles sold in Alba, the town they call the mecca of white truffles, come from nearby. The vast majority were probably hunted either in other parts of Italy or in eastern Europe." Frost, an ex-house DJ, founded the company after picking up the truffle bug while living in Tuscany. Having moved home to Wiltshire he read about a farmer who had truffles growing on his land and, after tasting them and becoming "obsessed", agreed hunting rights with him. "English truffles are awesome, but you can't compare them to winter truffles – it's like comparing a hatchback to a supercar," he says.

New sources have opened up, notably south-western Australia, which exports high-quality winter truffles during UK summertime while we wait for the same variety from Europe to arrive later in the year. Black autumn truffles were around £650 a kilo wholesale in November 2023, while the black winter Périgord variety was at least double that. A good fresh truffle should be firm and is highly perishable, needing refrigeration and eating as soon as possible after being dug up before it loses its perfume. If a truffle is immature, it might have no smell, and when over-ripe it develops a spongy texture and strong petrol aromas. They are available tinned, bottled and frozen, but these all lack the fragrance, texture and flavour of fresh. They are among the most pungent olfactory stimuli of any food – my kids won't stay in the same room when we eat white truffles. And I haven't even told them that in the Dark Ages, people used to think truffles grew out of witches' spit — or that the Spanish call truffles '*criadillas de tierra*', or earth testicles.

The best way to serve truffles is to shave them over bland food. Neither variety should be cooked, although infusing the more versatile black into other ingredients adds depth of flavour. Indeed, in Italy there's very little done with a valuable white truffle other than to shave it paper-thin, in as generous quantities as possible, over one of four simple dishes — buttered pasta, risotto, fonduta (a rich fondue of fontina cheese, milk, butter and eggs) or carne cruda (steak tartare) — before letting its magical fug invigorate the senses. I've heard contradictory opinions about what wine the Piedmontese drink alongside their truffles, with some saying they eschew their complex, mature Nebbiolos for simpler, fruity young Barberas and Dolcettos that don't get in the way of the aromas. I find this difficult to believe: a white truffle is always an occasion deserving of a special wine, no matter where you live.

"My favourite way to eat white truffle is over fried eggs with a classic Barolo," says Giampiero Cordero, whose restaurant Il Centro di Priocca is among the finest in Piedmont. "Many people think classic Barolo — rather than single vineyard crus — are 'entry-level' wines, when in reality they merge all the different characteristics that you can find in the area. A Barolo from La Morra may have an elegant perfume with fresher notes, and Serralunga more austerity and power, but a Barolo Classico creates a balanced wine with complexity, austerity and finesse, which is why I think it goes best with truffle." Like other local restaurateurs, Cordero sells truffle at a low margin almost as a courtesy, pulling visitors to the region. In nearby Barolo town, Carlotta Rinaldi also cites fried eggs and tajarin (local hand-cut pasta) as her dream accompaniments, with the mother lode of Barolo. "I've great memories of a truffle menu and old Barolos from Bartolo Mascarello, Giacomo Conterno and my family's wines," she says. "1958 Mascarello with eggs cocotte and truffle is stuck in my mind." Mature Brunello di Montalcino, Chianti, red/white Burgundies, and Champagne are all wines that can pair fantastically with white truffles, often developing musky, mushroomy perfumes that mirror and complement the truffle's.

At home, my recipe for truffle pasta (for four) is simple. Bring a pot of salted water to the boil and cook 400g of dried tagliolini as per instructions. Melt 70g of the finest unsalted butter possible over a low heat, add 50ml of white wine and turn up the heat to reduce by half. Turn the heat down and season with salt, pepper and nutmeg. When the pasta's done don't over-drain it, and dress with the warm butter sauce. Mix in 40g of grated Parmigiano Reggiano cheese, and divide on individual plates. Slice a clean white truffle as thinly as possible in front of your guests: 10g is an 'appropriate' serving, but better to double or triple that and open the most exhilarating wine you can lay your hands on — an old Montevertine 'Le Pergole Torte', say, or a Bruno Giacosa Barolo 'Le Rocche del Falletto' Riserva. Baked Vacherin Mont d'Or is also a joy covered in shaved white truffle, the two coming into season around the same time as each other.

Home cooks can be more creative with black truffles than white. If you're not sure you've ever tried them, but have dined at top starred restaurants you'll recognise their undertones because some add them to almost everything. "Black truffle gives a magical aroma by doing something as simple as grating it in a pan with a little warm butter, or adding to mash potato," says Brett Graham of Notting Hill's The Ledbury. "When you're infusing them into fat—cream, milk, butter—the flavour goes through the whole thing nicely and smells amazing. White truffles can smell strong and heady when you first take a whiff, whereas black are powerful but have a gentle, earthy, mushroomy flavour."

In southern France, Châteauneuf-du-Pape with Périgord truffles is a happy traditional combination, as is aromatic Condrieu. But then, why not a mature Roulot Meursault 'Les Luchets' with a truffled omelette, or an aged Krug Champagne with scrambled eggs on sourdough with black truffle generously grated over the top? Decadent, no doubt, but you're a long time dead. "My Boxing Day treat was an old-fashioned croque monsieur with a healthy amount of butter, honey-baked ham and béchamel sauce with black truffle, which I ate in front of the TV," says Graham. "That's a death-row dish for me—simple things go well."

If you've never eaten truffles, go in on one with pals for an extraordinary treat. As the irascible old star of *The Truffle Hunters* says: "Eggs, or anchovies and garlic, are good with truffles; if you aren't picky, you can eat them on anything!" ●

17

THE YEASTIE BOYS

*The return of non-fortified Sherries,
Sanlúcar de Barrameda, Spain*

Ramiro Ibáñez,
Alejandro
Muchada and
Willy Pérez,
Sanlúcar de
Barrameda, Spain.

If you were restricted to using a single adjective to describe Sanlúcar de Barrameda's Bodegas Barbadillo, you may well settle on 'historic'. With its vast regiments of old oak *botas* stacked in dimly lit high vaults next to the Atlantic, this cathedral of Sherry has seen little in the way of changes in the past 200 years. Even before then the region was a wildly successful exporter of the ubiquitous 'Sack' — as Sherry was known in ye very olden days — but now a feeling of faded glory pervades. You could call it a local speciality; the nearby port of Cádiz is where Sir Francis Drake incinerated a slumbering Armada, and from where Columbus set sail to the Americas. But while Barbadillo has timeless beauty, akin to a working museum, it offers nothing to suggest that Sherry is on the brink of a popular revival, as aficionados sometimes moot. "Prices are low and the history is big," Barbadillo cellar master Armando Guerra tells me over one of its sublime old Amontillados; happy days, indeed, for thrifty drinkers. But every wine needs a future. So, the question is: where will Sherry, a complex array of fortified styles at odds with modern trends for terroir-expression and moderate alcohol, be in 50 years' time?

Many of the signs are ominous. Sherry was once among the UK's most popular imports but production has decreased by a third since the turn of the millennium, with year-on-year sales graphs resembling the Winter Olympics' giant slalom course. For many people it's too confusing, too alcoholic, too full of the bizarre spirit-like chemical compound acetaldehyde (from biological ageing under *flor*), and too much like what their

nans — rather than their switched-on pals — want to drink. But while quantities are falling, some, like Barbadillo and the influential Equipo Navazos, have been doubling down on quality, sourcing rare *botas* from the region's treasure troves of ancient wines to release as hyper-specific one-off bottlings, and attracting an authenticity-thirsty audience through non-filtered *en rama* styles. Just as importantly, a new generation of *vignerons* is recovering Sherry's lost focus on origin, lesser-known native grapes, and vintage — rather than the ubiquitous fractional blending of multiple years in soleras — as well as the niche, but potentially seminal, renaissance of non-fortified wines.

Back in Elizabethan times all Sack was unfortified and naturally around 16% ABV (achieved by partially dehydrating grapes using *asoleo*, a sun-drying technique, or late harvesting); it wasn't until the 17th century that grape spirit was first added to help preserve the wines on long voyages to Britain and the New World. Even 150 years ago many of the best Sherries were not fortified, a time when eminent bodegas such as Domecq still promoted origin and farming rather than just the winery ageing processes that define styles such as Fino, Amontillado, Oloroso and Cream, which still dominate the modern industry. But change, no matter how small, has come and in 2021 new EU laws were passed permitting unfortified wines (of above 15% ABV) and a wider range of indigenous grapes to be classified as Sherry in the Manzanilla de Sanlúcar and Jerez-Xérès-Sherry DOPs. Two of the main producers lobbying for these changes were Willy Pérez of Bodegas Luis Pérez, and Ramiro Ibáñez of Bodegas Cota 45. Having spent the past decade researching the archives of great Sherry companies, they produce brilliant unfortified wines that reference the past while remaining grounded in the present.

"When we were growing up we saw Sherry as more like a spirit which, as lovers of terroir wines, didn't really appeal," says Pérez. "But we're not outsiders, or revolutionaries, as some people think — we're showing respect. We love the histories of bodegas like Domecq and González Byass, which are the reason we're even making wine today." Like their contemporaries in Ribeira Sacra, Tenerife, Catalonia et al., Pérez and Ibáñez are part of

Alejandro
Muchada, Muchada-
Léclapart,
Sanlúcar de
Barrameda.

an Andalusian contingent reclaiming lost traditions, helping make Spain arguably the most exciting wine country in the world today. Indeed, unfortified Sherries such as Luis Pérez's 2013 Fino 'Corregidor' Carrascal are a revelation; 'Fino' may mean 'refined', but few come close to this wine's combination of finesse and density. Likewise, Bodegas Cota 45's intense single-vineyard crus 'Maina' and 'Miraflores' are gold for mineral lovers, although their circa 12% ABVs mean they forgo Sherry DOP status.

A thirst for unfortified wines — a.k.a. mosto — has long been part of bar culture in Sanlúcar de Barrameda, where premises displayed a red flag when it was available to drink. Although mosto — or 'must' — means pre-fermentation grape juice in most other regions, here it means pre-fortification wine, with the first batches of the year arriving from the co-op and local cellars in November, much like Beaujolais Nouveau. Barbadillo was the first bodega to have commercial success with an unfortified wine from 1968, although it wasn't until 1975 that its 'Castillo de San Diego' brand was officially recognised (earlier vintages display 'This product is not authorised by the Consejo Regulador' on the label). A clean, simple white that the bodega sells for an astonishing €3.95 per bottle, 'Castillo de San Diego' has little to recommend about it, other than that it's wet and alcoholic. The first unfortified 'fine' wine — i.e. one with more distinctive qualities — wouldn't come until the late 2000s, when Douro *vigneron* Dirk Niepoort, who was successfully producing unfortified table wines alongside traditional fortified Port in his home region, suggested to Equipo Navazos that it take a similar approach.

Perhaps it was my fourth or fifth tasting at a Sherry bodega when I began losing all my usual bearings about what I was putting in my mouth, due to the lack of any vineyard, or vintage, information. But that was quickly remedied by Equipo Navazos' co-founder Eduardo Ojeda. Among the first of Sherry's elder statesmen to promote the idea of terroir, Ojeda and partner Jesús Barquín are pushing single-vineyard crus further with 'La Bota de Florpower', another excellent unfortified Palomino from Sanlúcar's Miraflores, as well as its ground-breaking Niepoort collaboration. "Nobody understood the first Navazos-Niepoort 2008 release," says Ojeda. "They weren't used to the style for a table wine — it was too mineral, too dry, too grippy. We had a lot of trouble selling it." Still niche propositions, these whites — as well as the debut 2018 Cask Fermented 'Macharnudo' by Valdespino, where Ojeda also works as technical director — subtly meld the spirit-esque tang of acetaldehyde from months, rather than years, of ageing under *flor*, with mineral details from the chalky albariza soils. "*Flor* is important, but terroir is the secret," says Ojeda. "I prefer those bodegas where you taste the vineyards."

Sanlúcar de Barrameda's albariza soils are nutritionally poor but retain water well, slowly releasing it to the region's swathes of Palomino and other indigenous vines during the dry summer months; a huge benefit even if the coastal breezes make the microclimate here significantly cooler than in nearby Cádiz and Seville. Interestingly, the town has drawn acclaimed Champagne grower David Léclapart — another master of chalk — to set up a fine-wine project in its backstreets with business partner Alejandro Muchada. Becoming friends when Muchada worked harvest at Léclapart in the Montagne de Reims, the pair bought 3ha of vineyards in the historic *pago* of Miraflores together in 2015, releasing Muchada-Léclapart's debut

vintage in 2016. "When we were searching for vineyards to buy David said we should look for beauty, as it would give a beautiful wine," says Muchada, a former architect from Cádiz who, like his pal, lets his artistic sensibilities inform his craft. Far from modern 'technical' winemaking, Muchada learnt his métier from Sanlúcar's elder *vignerons*, with his and Léclapart's salty 'Univers' and 'Lumière' having little to no *flor* influence.

Terroir-specific Palominos like these are attracting new drinkers to Sherry who could then go on to delve into its rich fortified history, which itself has new blood coming to the fore. At Bodegas Williams & Humbert, *vigneronne* Paola Medina is pioneering a range of vintage Sherries that forgo soleras, while Peter Sisseck — founder of Dominio de Pingus, one of Spain's most acclaimed cult estates — purchased Bodega San Francisco Javier with the Del Rio family of Hacienda Monasterio in 2017. "Peter rang me up to say how excited he was about buying the bodega, and that it felt like owning a Goya — owning history," recalls Carlos del Rio Jr. "But he also said that to make it sustainable we had to think long term and maintain the Goya for 15 years." That someone as savvy as Sisseck has become co-custodian of such extraordinary Andalusian heritage, while understanding that its commercial fortunes won't regenerate overnight, says much. If Sherry can balance its signature biological ageing with a return to quality farming and terroir- and vintage-specific bottlings, only the brave, or the myopic, would bet against its continuing relevance. As Eduardo Ojeda tells me over a 1948 Valdespino Amontillado with as much command of light and shade as any Old Master: "I don't want to focus on the *flor*, I want to taste the wine." ●

A SHORTCUT TO DRINKING GREAT SHERRY

Unfortified	Fortified
Muchada-Léclapart 'Lumière' $$$	Lustau '3 En Rama' Manzanilla $$
Bodegas Cota 45 Ube 'Miraflores' $$-$$$	Bodega San Francisco Javier 'Viña Corrales' Pago Balbaina Fino $$
Bodegas Cota 45 Ube 'Maina' $$-$$$	Bodegas Tradición VORS 30 Years Amontillado $$$-$$$$
Bodegas Luis Pérez 'Villamarta' $$-$$$	Williams & Humbert Williams Colección Añadas 'Tiento' Fino $$
M. Antonio de la Riva 'La Riva' Macharnudo $$-$$$	Equipo Navazos 'La Bota de Oloroso 94' $$$

18

WINE RATED BY ITS ALCOHOLIC EFFECTS

Not all bottles leave you feeling the same way

For all the adjective-addled impressions and analogies written about wine over the years, far fewer words have been dedicated to the effect of one of its most intrinsic components – alcohol. Which is surprising, given that while describing the evanescent sensations of smell and taste is a near-impossible task, the warm buzz of booze is easily conveyed. Of course, wine's dizzying array of people, places, grapes and flavours makes it endlessly fascinating. But would you be quite so fascinated if it didn't make the mundane morph into the bleeding marvellous by the end of the first glass? Wine helps everything feel Zen. Or rather, the right amount of the right wine makes you feel mighty righteous. For its myriad styles are far from equal, and whether it's 7% ABV 'breakfast' Riesling Kabinett, 16.5% Amarone or mass-manufactured toilet cleaner, different types of vino have very different effects.

Here's what I've learnt about ABV (alcohol by volume): the difference the next day between polishing off, say, a 12.5% Chinon from the Loire Valley, and that bottle of 16.5% Amarone, is the difference between feeling like a normal human being, or like the Manson family is smoking crack in your head. A few extra degrees in alcohol might not sound much, but drinking Amarone and its steroid-laden chums Aglianico, Primitivo or Châteauneuf-du-Pape is the oenological equivalent of being spiked with Rohypnol. Of course, any benefits from avoiding a bruising ABV are wiped out if you are drinking aforementioned toilet cleaner. Because, as everyone

knows (and I stand by this entirely non-scientific fact) QUALITY WINE
DOES NOT GIVE YOU A HANGOVER. Poundland Zinfandel, on the other
hand, is the gateway to the ninth circle of hell.

But I'm no angsty puritan; I simply haven't found many wines naturally
reaching 16.5% ABV that I want to put in my mouth. By all means please
pour me a fortified 19%+ ABV Amontillado – but I'll savour a small glass,
not suffer a whole bottle of Château Deranged that'll melt my brain. A
century ago, when grapes often failed to fully ripen in the pre-apocalyptic
climate, *vignerons* equated high alcohol content with high quality. Today
harvesting ripe fruit is not a problem in regions such as Burgundy and
Bordeaux, so it's not how much alcohol you can produce, but how you moderate it, that's in vogue. Unless, of course, you've the taste for ramped-up
tramp juice and, like some of my friends, base your wine purchases mainly
on how much booze they contain.

So what other styles should the canny wino look for? Well, it's been said
that drinking too much Bordeaux makes for a bad drunk because it makes
you believe everything you say is really important – and certainly I've met
a few château-owners who sound as if they're on the Colombian marching
powder. If we're talking really BAD DRUNK, you might want to consider
that Alexander the Great killed his best friend Cleitus while out together
on the ancient Hellenic sauce. Fortunately, Greek wines such as the now
very on-trend Xinomavro have improved immeasurably over the past two-
and-a-half millennia, their reputation as ancestral firewater replaced by
a propensity for somnolence. Which is a far preferable end to an evening
than having your servants drop a pal off at the morgue. For my money, old-
school claret ('80s bottles typically weigh in at a modest 12.5% ABV) provides among the most measured merriness of any red – the player's choice
for a cheeky midweek lunch when required to be vaguely able to operate
heavy machinery by supper.

The alcoholic effects of sweet wine – especially in a situation such as
Hardy Rodenstock's legendary 1998 tasting of 125 vintages of Château
d'Yquem, where many guests never spat – poses different questions. Such
as: can you even get drunk on that much Sauternes before diabetes kicks
in? As for Port, which should definitely be limited to a single glass, I say
NO THANKS. One Christmas Eve many moons ago, its saccharine taste
lured me in with a false sense of security, then confined me to bed for the
whole of the following day. Give me the giddiness of top Meursault and
Puligny-Montrachet, and the sheer elation of Burgundian Pinot Noir. The
best brings on consciousness-expanding experiences that make a drinker
laugh out loud with delight (there are rumours that the EU is considering reclassifying Chambolle-Musigny Premier Cru 'Les Amoureuses' as
a class B drug).

Talking of drugs, is there any purer anti-anxiety medication than the
finest sulphur-free wines? I defy anyone to drink Joško Gravner's whole-
some Ribolla, Thierry Allemand's soulful Cornas, or soothing Beaujolais
from the cup of Domaine Lapierre, and keep a smile as wide as the Channel
Tunnel from their face. So much tastier than Xanax. Likewise, stony-fresh
Tuscan Sangiovese is a dependable provider of goodwill to all – except,
perhaps, my wife, who says that my contented snoring after a bellyful of
Soldera can wake up our street. Ditto Stella di Campalto happy-juice. In
the perfect world, great Sangiovese would be available for all on the NHS.

Selosse
'Substance'
solera, Avize,
Champagne.

But if I had to choose just one wine to keep for its effects, it would undoubtedly be weapons-grade Champagne. From the pop of the cork to the bead of tiny bubbles mainlining happiness into my bloodstream, it's always a crystalline high. Whether it's Vouette et Sorbée's salty Aube fizz or golden Krug 1959, life's possibilities seem endless in Champagne's glow. To paraphrase Henry Vizetelly's 1882 celebration *A History of Champagne*, it can enliven the dullest reunion, soften the sternest cynic, sate the most irascible temper, and loosen the most taciturn tongue. It promotes light-heartedness and can, some say, comfort the sick. Of course, I realise how hopelessly out of touch it sounds rhapsodising over spenny bubbles, so I'll take a bow and leave all you Amarone lovers out there with my hangover cure. Châteldon water, Dioralyte and a swim followed by a glass of Selosse 'Substance' takes some beating. ●

19

BEYOND BUBBLES

Fizz-free winemaking in Coteaux Champenois, Champagne, France

Aube vineyards, southern Champagne, France.

My son Arthur has good questions. "Dad, why does this wine cost — gasp! — £200, and others £10?" he asked, pointing to a bottle of Château l'Église-Clinet. It was a request for clarity that should feature regularly in the minds of all wine lovers. "Well, this is a rare bottle made by a renowned producer," I replied, introducing the lad to the mad world of wine prices. "And see this word on the label — P.O.M.E.R.O.L? That's a special area that makes beautiful reds that feel like velvet in your mouth." In that context, £200 is a fair tariff for such a venerable wine. But had Arthur pointed to the bottle on which I spent almost the same in order to research Coteaux Champenois — 2018 Louis Roederer 'Hommage à Camille' Blanc — and asked the same, I would've read out the letters C.O.T.E.A.U.X C.H.A.M.P.E.N.O.I.S and said, "This is a rare still wine from a place and producer that makes extraordinary fizz, but where the still wines vary wildly from thin and mean to big and oaky. God knows why it costs so much money."

Given Roederer's pedigree, I'd assumed that I'd be able to regale you with plaudits for the first fruit of its Coteaux Champenois project. But after following this still Le Mesnil-sur-Oger Chardonnay over consecutive days (I've never drunk anything so slowly), the best I can muster is "meh". If wine's most important purpose is to provide pleasure, this vapid adolescent demanded to be taken seriously yet offered no seduction. Besides, if you can buy two bottles of Dauvissat Chablis Premier Cru 'La Forest' — a still white with oodles more energy and dimension from a relatively nearby benchmark AOC — or one bottle of Roederer's never less than brilliant Cristal for the same moolah, why on earth would you bother?

But 'Hommage à Camille' aside, there are good reasons for rising interest in Coteaux Champenois. Not only did ye olde still wines of Champagne fuel French kings' coronations years before Dom Pérignon's mythical discovery of *la Méthode Champenoise* (and improved glassmaking produced bottles capable of withstanding the pressure of the secondary fermentation), but rising temperatures mean that the region may soon be able to ripen still wines to rival their Burgundian cousins to the south. (And in time, following a similar trajectory north, perhaps us Brits too.) Sure, these rare positive effects of climate change might make a compelling story, but after tasting many Coteaux Champenois it's clear that Domaine de la Romanée-Conti may sleep easily for a few harvests yet.

Known from the early days of the appellation system as Vin Ordinaire de la Champagne Viticole, then Vin Nature de la Champagne from 1953 to 1974, Coteaux Champenois production has shrunk from four million bottles in the early '80s to 80,000 today. To say it's niche is like calling the Mongol Horde 'a little pushy'. Indeed, with many *cuvées* released as just a few hundred bottles, it is a tiny, fairly uncommercial consideration in wineries' portfolios. But with many young Champenois enrolling in wine school in Burgundy, or visiting regularly to taste, their fascination with terroir-specific still Chardonnays and Pinot Noirs is growing. The fact remains, however, that only Champagne Grands Crus in the warmest years can ripen grapes anywhere close to the natural potential alcohol level needed to make compelling still wines (an estimated 60% of all vines in the region are harvested at under 10% ABV). So adding sugar and yeast to create a second fermentation, and blending vintage variations, remains route one for vinous pleasure.

Climate is not the only thing limiting the ability to make world-class still wine here. Most vineyards are planted with clones adept at producing Champagne's famously high yields (60 to 80 hectolitres per hectare) compared with top Burgundy's more quality-oriented ones (regularly below 40hl/ha from vines often planted via *sélection massale*). Then there's the question of whether the terroir — Champagne's high proportion of chalky soils and different exposures and altitudes — is suitable. Not to mention distinct winemaking sensibilities. Rodolphe Péters, of Le Mesnil-sur-Oger's Champagne Pierre Péters, told me of his ambition to make still wines, but acknowledged that many underestimate the challenge, assuming it to be roughly the same as producing *vin clair* (low-alcohol pre-secondary fermentation still wines). "When you speak with the Burgundians about how they make wine, you realise it's a totally different mindset," he says.

But is it fair comparing Coteaux Champenois with Burgundy, France's long-established champion of still reds and whites? As both grow Pinot Noir and Chardonnay, sit near each other, and are sold at a premium prices (due to Coteaux Champenois' high costs of harvesting low yields from expensive land), it's difficult not to. But while the consistency of Côte d'Or wines has improved since the turn of the millennium (it's now very rare to find under-ripe wines, even if many are still chaptalised) it's unrealistic to expect the same from Champagne's more marginal climate, and relatively inexperienced still winemakers. As a Champagne lover, I really want to like these wines, but after sifting through 25 different Coteaux Champenois that averaged between £80 and £100 a bottle, it was a spendy review of an appellation that remains a work in progress. Some, such as

Bollinger's 2016 'La Côte aux Enfants' and Henri Giraud's 2014 Aÿ Blanc 'Cuvée de Croix Courcelles', covered a lack of underlying dimension with new oak, while others, such as Stroebel's inaccurately named 2018 Le Vin Tranquille 'Les Paquis', were volatile and and full of brettanomyces. Still, there were also glimmers of gold in the tilted pan.

Tasting so many Coteaux Champenois showed how stylistically diverse the appellation is, and my favourite reds were poles apart. Egly-Ouriet's benchmark Ambonnay Rouge 'Cuvée des Grands Côtés' Vieilles Vignes was another wine that wore its *élevage* in Burgundian barrels heavily – although, to be honest, I'm quite partial to expensive oak provided there's something interesting beneath. The 2018 has no shortage of flavour or body – a powerful, spicy wine that might appeal to Californian Pinot lovers – while the svelte 2017 had an exotic rose-petal perfume and silky tannins. Francis Egly undertakes a severe green harvest on 60+ year-old vines in Ambonnay, late-harvesting very low yields to make these wines. Roger Coulon is another family domaine in nearby Vrigny increasing quality through regenerative farming and thoughtful winemaking, making the impressive (and unusual 100% whole bunch Pinot Meunier) Coteaux Champenois 'Le Mont Moine'. It's a harmonious red with a tobacco-spice, sappy whole-bunch perfume that makes you feel like you're among the vines.

Aurélien Lurquin's organic vineyards, full of *sélection massale* old vines, are well-suited for still wine. Lurquin specialises in still wines of all colours as well as sparkling, and is a star of the natural scene. Perhaps this is as much to do with the scarcity of his wine as the quality: the characterful 2019 Coteaux Champenois 'Les Forcières' was released in a grand total of 260 bottles and 18 magnums. Echo Falls this ain't. A poised red with fine powdery tannins and aromas of violets and undergrowth, it had no hint of the under-ripeness that plagued many of the *cuvées* I tasted. Likewise his rare 2020 'Les Forcières' rosé, which is a beautiful wine. Perhaps that shouldn't be surprising given that the region's third appellation – after AOCs Champagne and Coteaux Champenois – is Rosé des Riceys, located in the south, which specialises in the style. The master here is Olivier Horiot, whose Rosé des Riceys and 2018 Coteaux Champenois Riceys Blanc 'En Valingrain' – a smoky, tarragon-cut white wine – are outstanding.

Bérêche has become one of my favourite Champagne producers, and it was fascinating to see the gains that Raphaël and his brother Vincent have made with their Coteaux Champenois 'Les Montées' Rouge from its debut 2009 vintage to the more refined 2019. Even more impressive were their Coteaux Champenois 'Les Monts Fournois' Ludes Premier Cru Blanc 2014 and 2016 – small productions of massale-selected Chardonnay from southern-exposed chalk vineyards planted in 1961. Both have good intensity, the 2016 majoring on preserved citrus, flowers and salty minerals. "We can make good still wines in Champagne but our biggest challenge is finding suitable old parcels of vines, as all the growers for the big houses replanted theirs with clones decades ago," says Rapha. "My dream is to continue developing our experimental *bibliothèque* of terroirs, so that in the future our children can look back and see if it is a good or bad idea." ●

A SHORTCUT TO DRINKING GREAT COTEAUX CHAMPENOIS
& ROSÉ DES RICEYS

Roger Coulon
Coteaux Champenois
'Le Mont Moine'
$$$

Egly-Ouriet
Coteaux Champenois
Ambonnay Rouge 'Cuvée des Grands Côtés'
Vieilles Vignes
$$$$

Aurélien Lurquin
Coteaux Champenois
'Les Forcières' Rosé
$$$$

Bérêche et Fils
Coteaux Champenois
'Les Monts Fournois' Ludes Premier
Cru Blanc
$$$

Olivier Horiot
Rosé des Riceys
'En Barmont'
$$$

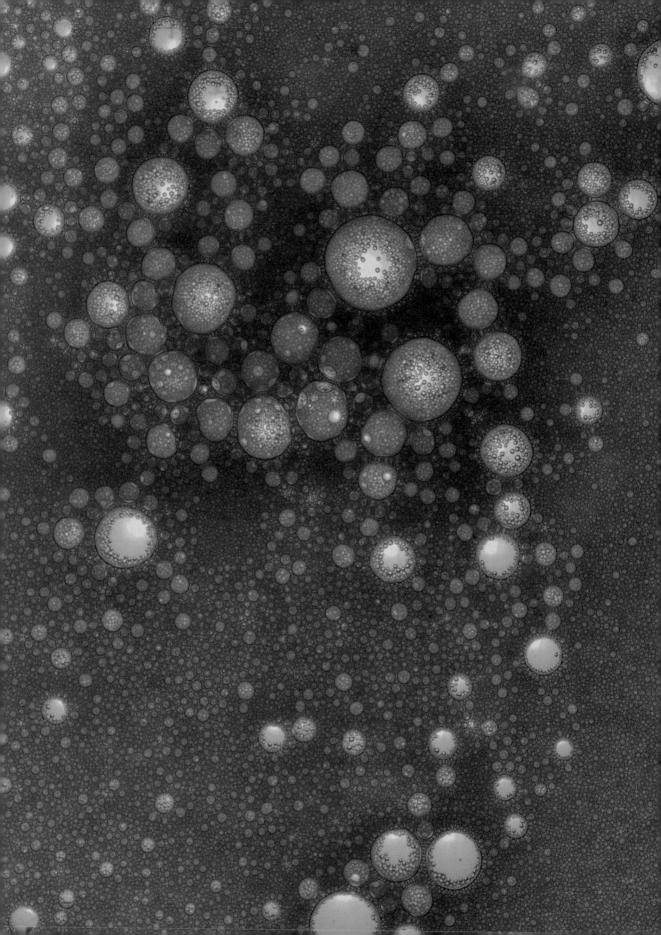

20

CHAMPAGNE'S WORST-KEPT SECRET

Getting serious about sparkling rosé,
Champagne, France

Close-up of rosé
Champagne bubbles
taken through a
macro lens.

Does there come a time in every man's life when he looks at his cellar and says to himself: "I need a £39,000 gold-plated methuselah of 1996 Dom Pérignon Rosé"? I can't be alone in this, surely. A few years ago the Champagne house named for the flamboyant monk released 35 such oversized bottles, which, according to one website, rather grandly require that 'sommeliers use white silk gloves to open or pour the contents'. But, short of remortgaging my house, or selling the car, I'm coming to terms with the fact that their rather less glitzy regular rosé is the closest I'll come to overcoming my mid-life crisis.

It's difficult enthusing about fine wine at the best of times without sounding like the over-privileged love child of Imelda Marcos and Winston Churchill, but especially so given one of my guiltiest pleasures: rosé Champagne. Like so many Brits, once summer arrives I default to drinking still rosé in my garden while dreaming of a smallholding in Provence. But whereas we only really drink still rosé in the sun, I love the fizzy variety all year round, appreciating everything about it: its effervescence, its vinosity, and its aromatic echoes of red Burgundy. I'm in the minority, though. Because after decades of the type of advertising that would do a Pyongyang brainwashing facility proud convinced the world that Champagne is for special occasions, to serve the lesser-spotted pink variety is still a source of doubt.

Why do so many drinkers not consider rosé Champagne a 'serious' fine wine worthy of contemplation like Burgundy or Bordeaux? Perhaps because it's been tarred with commercial still rosé's frivolous image — it

Pierre Baillette
'Bulles Roses'
Champagne.

doesn't take the FBI to deduce that Whispering Angel is about as authentic as one of Rudy Kurniawan's 1949 Ponsots. Maybe it's down to the genre's rarity – though rosé production has risen from 2% of Champagne's annual output in 1980 to circa 10% today. Or that many drinkers consider the price uplift between Grandes Marques' white and rosé *cuvées* as pure marketing. But although pimped-up methuselahs are a reflection of the strange outer reaches of society's wealthiest, there are many more accessible rosé Champagnes deserving of your attention.

Pierre Baillette, a microgrower domaine in Trois-Puits, south of Reims, is a great place to start. Périne Baillette produces two rosés using the two techniques permitted by EU law. 'Le Village' is a lighter style made via the most common method of 'assemblage', where a small amount of still red is blended with a base white before secondary fermentation. And 'Bulles Roses' is 100% Pinot Noir made using the *saignée* method, where black grapes are left to macerate on the skins for a short time to take on a pink hue before being 'bled' off into a fermentation tank. *Saignée*-method Champagnes tend to be more structured than blends, soaking up tannins from the skins and pips.

Two other excellent examples, which couldn't be more different, are Vouette et Sorbée's minimal sulphur 'Saignée de Sorbée' from the Aube (which can vary from a darkish wine with a rustic perfume of cured meats and spice to a finer, more conventional red-fruited light pink, depending on the vintage) and Louis Roederer Brut Nature, an elegant, salmon-coloured fizz that tastes of strawberries and cream but, due to no extra *dosage*, has a pleasingly austere finish. Louis Roederer is widely respected for converting its large number of vineyards to biodynamics, and is one of the few using the *saignée* method to make rosé, including for its sublime Cristal Rosé.

Unfortunately, the vast majority of other Champagne vineyards are still farmed using dubious methods. But what a higher-quality rosé Champagne can offer beyond a white one, besides the obvious differences in colour, are red Burgundy-esque aromas of strawberries, roses, undergrowth, and exotic spice, and a little extra body that can stand up to some meat dishes. Some go even further, such as Jacques Selosse Brut Rosé – another of my 'death-row' wines – a *sui generis* Sherry-like fizz that blends a small percentage of still red bought from top grower Egly-Ouriet into immaculate Avize Chardonnay. Imagine mature Krug with a Vin Jaune top and you're halfway there.

Krug, of course, does an inimitable job of its own rosé. As does Billecart-Salmon, whose standard rosé is a nailed-on crowd-pleaser that, again, tastes just like wild strawberries. Besides the understated methuselahs, out of all the big houses, Dom Pérignon undeniably makes one of the most pleasurable rosés – its attention to detail impressive given the scale of its production. 1988 Dom Pérignon rosé is an all-time classic, its woozy bubbles quickly dissipating to leave a zesty, spicy, saline broth of mellow perfection in their wake. The glimmer of Champagne with the umami depths of Chambertin? Shhh! There's not THAT much to go around. ●

A SHORTCUT TO DRINKING GREAT ROSÉ CHAMPAGNE

Jacques Selosse
Brut Rosé
$$$$

Billecart-Salmon
'Elisabeth Salmon' Rosé
$$$-$$$$

Vouette et Sorbée
'Saignée de Sorbée' Rosé
$$$

Dom Pérignon
Rosé
$$$$

BRILLIANT BUBBLES
CHAMPAGNE REIMAGINED

Jérôme Prévost
La Closerie 'Fac-Simile'
Extra Brut Rosé
$$$$

In 2017 I asked the owner of a well-
respected Grande Marque what he
thought of Pinot Meunier as a mono-
variety wine. Not much, he scoffed;
it was little more than an ingredient
used for adding body to non-vintage
blends. Three years later, his company
released its debut 100% Pinot Meunier
cuvée to great fanfare and a name so
hopelessly clichéd it would made Benny
Hill wince. Aside from other pioneers
like Egly-Ouriet and Françoise Bedel,
the Grandes Marques must have been
looking at Jérôme Prévost, who's long
crafted sublime, pure Pinot Meunier
bubbles in the village of Gueux on the
Petite Montagne de Reims. 'Fac-Simile'
is Prévost's tiny production rosé,
a blend of the one barrel of red he
makes from Pinot Meunier harvested in
a central 20-metre squared section
of his 'Les Béguines' vineyard, and
ten barrels of white. I adore its
harmony and depth — and how its
expressive aromatics remind me of
great red Burgundy.

Salon
Cuvée 'S' Le Mesnil Blanc de Blancs Brut
$$$$$

Eugène-Aimé Salon was an uncompromising chap. Like Gianfranco Soldera in Brunello di Montalcino years later, he broke so much ground that he established a new way of thinking about wine. Born in 1867 in Champagne's Côte des Blancs, Salon moved to Paris and became a furrier. But Salon dreamed of making Champagne instead of mink coats, and after surveying the region's most celebrated terroirs bought choice plots in Le Mesnil Grand Cru because of their wines' age-worthy characteristics. In 1905, he produced what he christened his debut 'Blanc de Blancs' — the first Champagne ever to be made purely of Chardonnay — reserving the full production, Prince de Conti style, for his own consumption (why not?). In 1920, after the First World War, Eugène-Aimé founded Salon and his innovative single-vineyard/vintage/cépage Champagnes became the toast of the Roaring Twenties.

Salon's standards have remained so high over the past century that it has deemed only 39 vintages good enough for release. And as with all wines that exacting, every bottle comes at a premium. Indeed, any opportunity to drink Salon with maturity and provenance is a rare joy — as unexpectedly happened to me a few years ago at the offices of its British agent, Corney & Barrow. I say unexpectedly, because the invite to the launch of 2004 Salon only mentioned one wine, not the embarrassment of riches laid on by Salon president Didier Depond for a handful of guests, and the 'self-service' accessibility of not only the '04 but the '02, '99, '97, '96, '90, '88, '71 and '66 too, in a heightened Christmas morning-like atmosphere. My taste buds did a little dance.

Drinking such wines with no prior warning was a revelation. Starting with the relatively tight and intense '04 and '02, whose Golden Delicious apple flavours combined with deep oxidative notes, the fireworks really started with the more mature '96's tarte tatin and Montrachet fragrance. The '88, another renowned vintage in Champagne, far surpassed expectations. Even though it had no bubbles (a common occurrence with very old 'sparkling' wine) its oxidative amalgamation of red apple, nuts, smoke, toffee and salt brought to mind a particularly magical Madeira. As did the '66 — after Depond swiftly replaced a first bottle that smelt like nail-varnish remover. But of all the Salons, the sublime '71 left the deepest impression. Dark golden-coloured and again devoid of bubbles, this time the scent was so exquisite it could've been the ghost of legendary French chef Fernand Point cooking tarte tatin, its almost endless finish ping-ponging between piquant apples and godly beef consommé.

21

A GOOD AND MOST PARTICULAR TASTE

Searching for individuality in Bordeaux, France

Château Les Carmes Haut-Brion, Péssac-Léognan, Bordeaux.

Most oenophiles, beside their common fondness for ritual and merriment, have an additional affinity with a particular region or style. For lovers of classical gastronomy, it might be the Northern Rhône Valley; for sulphur-dodgers the Jura; or for sadomasochists the most tooth-enamel-removing, unreconstructed Barolo that money can buy. Some, who prize ideology above all, pledge allegiance to the anti-establishment ethos of natural wine, where faults are forgiven at the altar of virtue. But incredible as it now seems, only a generation ago — before the tsunami of change that swept wine culture, making these and countless other regions and styles more accessible — the most coveted wine on the planet was Cru Classé claret. That's right kids — grandpa's yawn-some red Bordeaux.

Today a generation of switched-on drinkers wouldn't know a Château Lynch-Bages from a Langoa Barton — and have zero aspiration to drink either. Unlike millions before them, their introduction to serious vino wasn't reading Hugh Johnson's inspiring scribblings, or Robert Parker's game-changing reviews. Instead, they've scrolled upon an Instagram post featuring a bottle of Chenin Blanc with a fluorescent label that looked like a rave flyer; or partied in one of the legion 'natty' wine bars that have sprung up from Paris to Timbuktu. Indeed, the past decade has seen influencers — the French call them *prescripteurs* — not just pushing more dynamic niche regions, but actively discouraging people from buying what they see as overvalued, outmoded claret.

Bordeaux losing its crown had as much to do with its cringeworthy corporate tendencies as the accessibility of more innovative vineyards. Ironically, around the same time more drinkers were becoming fascinated by artisanal wines that embody traditional values, many châteaux were heading in the total opposite direction, with a cohort of hired-in consultants making richer, glossier, more concentrated generic styles aimed at critical acclaim. By the time of the 2009 and 2010 vintages' *en primeur* campaigns—the Bordelais' historic system for selling wine at low rates before bottling—a lively market, buoyed up by Hong Kong scrapping duty and Robert Parker publishing an unprecedented number of perfect scores, pushed demand to new highs. But, as the Bordelais price their wines according to the market rather than their intrinsic quality, the similarly expensive but much more average 2011s soon left a bad taste in drinkers' mouths.

Bordeaux *en primeur* is now a shadow of what it once was, and the prices of some mature vintages are among the most mystifying parts of an ever-more nonsensical fine-wine market. With top Burgundies and cult wines from Jura and Rhône now only affordable for the very wealthy, older Bordeaux actually looks—AND NEVER IN A MILLION VINTAGES DID I THINK I'D SAY THIS—great value. After all, it's not as if the qualities that made drinkers fall in love with claret in the first place—soothing flavours, reliability, and the mellow buzz of the restrained old-school style (something very in tune with today's trend for moderate alcohol)—have evaporated into thin air. Sure, the best Bordeaux requires at least 20 years to be at its most interesting, when slowly rotting fruit metamorphoses into joyful savouriness, but not only are such glass-ready beauts in bountiful supply, they're often only fractionally more expensive—and sometimes even cheaper—than nascent vintages. That the *en primeur* price of a dozen 2021 Cos d'Estournel was £200 more than the then-current price of 2001 Cos d'Estournel made as much sense as one of Bernie Madoff's hare-brained schemes.

But it's not just the money. While yesteryear's elegant Crus Classés provide easy pleasure, many of today's beefier, boozier, warm-climate reds provide little excitement. Part of old-school claret's charm lies in its imperfections, which many châteaux tried to eradicate in the pursuit of consistency and being 'the best'—although a new generation of winemakers is rethinking what the latter means. Bordeaux may be France's largest fine wine-producing region, but the gulf between the 100 or so Cru Classé châteaux that matter and several thousand small, obscure wineries that struggle for survival is stark. The individuality that is at the core of many dream wines of yore—be it mature vintages from salt-of-the-earth mavericks such as Domaine du Jaugaret and Château Bel-Air Marquis d'Aligre, or '59 Château Latour—is in danger of disappearing. Indeed, *Noble Rot* magazine's 'Essential Wines of the Decade' may not have included any Bordeaux at all if William Kelley hadn't nominated 2019 Château Troplong Mondot as an example of some first fruits of change.

So, what can the Bordelais do to become relevant to younger drinkers? Never mind 'fiddling while Rome burns'—with so much keenly priced mature wine in the market, does anyone seriously believe their annual *en primeur* echo chamber, where squads of critics and merchants are bussed around châteaux tasting two-year-old wines, will reignite interest? At least improvements in farming and a trend for elegant winemaking are happening. If a generation ago Bordeaux was focused far more on winery craft than viticulture, now it's the opposite—you can lose track of

the times châteaux explain that nowadays, they simply tip their grapes into a vat and let them infuse. Troplong Mondot, for its part, has implemented sweeping changes under new director Aymeric de Gironde, from decreasing the use of new oak, and going from being the last to the first château in St-Émilion to harvest its grapes, to paying attention to the maturity of its different parcels for more character and finesse. That grapes lose terroir definition when overly ripe is apparent when tasting 2015 and 2018 Troplong Mondot side by side: the previous regime's opaque, oaky 2015 – with glycerine-rich tears clinging to the sides of the glass like wallpaper paste – lacks the finesse and attractive fresh perfume of crushed coriander seeds of de Gironde's 2018.

To make such changes Troplong Mondot parted ways with Michel Rolland and his team – among the most successful consultants of the Parker years, when châteaux adapted to appeal to the influential critic's taste for excessively rich styles. Both Rolland and Parker were hugely effective communicators who shook up a region rife with complacency, even if their ideas about improving quality often masked many of the subtle characteristics that spoke of the wines' place of origin. Today, Thomas Duclos – a 40-something wine-loving oenologist who now advises Troplong Mondot and around 20 other Cru Classé châteaux – has more discriminating ideas. "Not long ago the idea was to make the best wine in each plot and then blend them, but now it's to harness the personality of each plot," says Duclos. "I prefer to paint a picture using many different colours, not just blue like 20 years ago. Now we also use red, green and yellow."

Identity, rather than 'quality' at all cost, is also the priority at Château Cheval Blanc, on the far side of St-Émilion. "We're not paid to make the best wine in Bordeaux each year, we're paid to deliver the best Cheval

Blanc," says technical director Pierre-Olivier Clouet, echoing similar aims to Duclos in its own 55 plots. A leader in regenerative farming (it's planted over 3,000 trees in its vineyards over the past five years and abandoned ploughing to protect biodiversity, for example), it takes its responsibility as one of Bordeaux's most celebrated châteaux seriously. "Ten years ago, we would've been fired for making these changes, but it's our duty to change people's minds," says Clouet. "Cheval Blanc planting trees isn't going to change the world, but it might influence other producers to do similar."

Cheval Blanc's extraordinarily luxurious texture sets it apart from most others. But given that, as Clouet himself says, its wine's "spirit appears after ten years", I wonder who'll actually drink recent vintages. Is Bordeaux's holy grail now to make reds that, like Burgundies, are enjoyable to drink soon after release 'on the fruit' but also capable of long-term ageing? At Château Canon, another Duclos client in St-Émilion prioritising precision, I visit exceptionally well-stocked cellars full of vintages dating back over a century and taste an effortless 2015 and 1940 – a so-called 'lesser' year that here produced a thought-provoking wine still full of energy and finesse. "I hope we're at least doing as good work today as what they were doing in the '40s," says Nicolas Audebert, another of the more creative winemakers in the region.

Bordeaux's price and drinking window may be in the spotlight, but in search of the missing individuality that has turned me and countless drinkers off, I drive to Château Haut-Brion in Graves, the birthplace of viticulture in the region. As the prototype classed-growth château that was first to sell wine under a brand name, it's also the inspiration for one of the most enduring tasting notes in history. In 1667, London diarist Samuel Pepys wrote of drinking a "sort of French wine, called Ho Bryan, that hath a good and most particular taste that I ever met with." Remarkably, some 350 years later Pepys' note is still on the money – a tribute to a unique terroir, and an unusually distinctive wine. Indeed, Haut-Brion is one of very few wines that I'd feel confident trying to identify at first sniff without seeing the label: the same tell-tale perfume of warm bricks, plasticine, tobacco and blackcurrants that first wowed me in the 1998, then later in legendary vintages such as '90, '89, '61 and '45, and is etched onto the pleasure receptors in my brain.

It's been said that producing great wine is akin to distilling a landscape into a glass. But on first look at Haut-Brion's vineyards one overcast winter afternoon, I'm surprised that this barren patch of moonscape, surrounded by the drab suburbs of Bordeaux city, grows anything at all. Jean-Philippe Delmas – the third successive generation of Delmas at the helm of Haut-Brion – explains how his grandfather replanted plots of Mourvèdre and Syrah in the '30s to conform to new appellation laws, and tells me about the five years and counting of renovations at the property that it hopes will set it up for the long haul.

"Haut-Brion is easy to sell," Delmas says, but I wonder if this will always be the case. How does it plan to attract the next generations of customers: people now at university drinking Mount Etna Nerello Mascalese, or Beaujolais Cru, who will one day have the means – but not necessarily the inclination – to buy expensive Bordeaux that requires long ageing before drinking? Even I, an established fan, wouldn't buy any Haut-Brion made in the past 15 years. Haut-Brion's characteristics may still run through

Pierre-Olivier
Clouet, Château
Cheval Blanc,
St-Émilion.

the heralded 2019, but you can buy that interstellar 1998 for not much more, and rising temperatures have taken alcohol from 13% to 14.6%. That might not sound much, but given that the 1998 is good to go now and for the next 30 years, and the 2019 is intrinsically brawnier and needs 30 years, I know which I'd choose.

One man who appears to have some of the answers is Guillaume Pouthier, director at neighbouring Château Les Carmes Haut-Brion. Here's a Bordeaux that drinks beautifully straight out of the blocks and offers something different. Historically, Haut-Brion is compared with its neighbour La Mission Haut-Brion — which Haut-Brion also acquired in 1983. But even though Les Carmes Haut-Brion is not a classed growth, includes a high percentage of fragrant Cabernet Franc, and uses an average of 50% whole clusters in fermentation with very passive extraction — something unprecedented in Bordeaux over recent decades — I would love to watch how this third neighbour's recent wine compares decades into the future.

What impresses me most about 2017 Château Les Carmes Haut-Brion isn't just that it has that 'most particular' Graves perfume of warm bricks and tobacco, or that its fine tannins and restrained alcohol make it a joy to drink even at such an early stage. It's that Pouthier and château-owner Patrice Pichet have had the nerve to do something different. When many other producers said that including stems (a technique most famously used at Domaine de la Romanée-Conti in Burgundy, and in the Northern Rhône, where Pouthier previously worked for Chapoutier) would lead to unattractive vegetal aromas, it followed its convictions and, after years of perfecting the method, is making wines that not only go nose-to-nose with the best in the country, but do it on their own terms. Picking a little earlier and including stems in a special method of infusion means Les Carmes Haut-Brion averages 13.5% ABV compared to 14.5% or 15% next door.

"It's easy to get good extraction today, so it's about doing less," says Pouthier, a man who I sense can hardly contain his excitement for his métier. "I'm always saying to my team 'do less' in the winery. You wait and you do nothing." If anything, these wines remind me of a hypothetical cross between Haut-Brion and Clos Rougeard Saumur-Champigny 'Le Bourg' — a pure Cabernet Franc from the Loire. These are highly perfumed, easy-to-drink, yet elegantly structured reds, with an individuality that sets them as far apart from other clarets as Château Rayas is from other Châteauneuf-du-Papes. Might other Bordeaux producers adopt similar methods to hold back rising alcohol levels and promote freshness? Or will they worry that they stand to lose more by trying to change, and carry on as they always have? As the old saying goes, the only things guaranteed in life are death and taxes. Not even Bordeaux *en primeur*. ●

A SHORTCUT TO DRINKING GREAT BORDEAUX

Domaine de Galouchey
'Le Galouchey'
Vin de France
$$$

Château Canon
St-Émilion
$$$-$$$$

Château Cheval Blanc
St-Émilion
$$$$-$$$$$

Vieux Château Certan
Pomerol
$$$-$$$$

Château Montrose
St-Estèphe
$$$-$$$$

Château Les Carmes Haut-Brion
Pessac-Léognan
$$$-$$$$

Château Haut-Brion
Pessac-Léognan
$$$$-$$$$$

POWER OF LA FLOWER
THE MAGIC OF POMEROL'S CHÂTEAU LAFLEUR

A modest property neighbouring world-beating Pétrus, Château Lafleur can be every bit as magical on its day. Indeed this 'garden vineyard' in Pomerol, an appellation that only gained its present-day notoriety after the war, grows one of Gaul's greatest reds, a wine that blossoms after decades in the cellar. Lafleur's longevity owes something to its unusually high proportion of Cabernet Franc compared with other Merlot-dominated Pomerols, the former adding aromatic complexity, the latter opulent, velveteen body.

Owned by the Guinaudeau family, Lafleur feels more like a classic Côte d'Or domaine than a slick Bordelais château. And the wines — Jesus Christ the wines! — are some of the most profound I've ever tasted. Lafleur 1982 far surpasses anything you could rightfully expect from 'fermented grape juice', its visceral sense of restrained power matched by its lacy finesse. The 1975, the finest of my birth year, was explosive and muscular, only beginning to reveal its pleasures. 1966 — another wow! — with a sensational floral nose, just like the 1964, whose sweet scent combines coriander and rose. Lastly, the 1950 stakes a case for its immortality, an incredibly intense and youthful wine.

VINTAGE VARIATIONS
OR WHY A SUPERIOR WINE FROM A BADLY RATED VINTAGE IS MORE GRATIFYING
THAN AN INFERIOR WINE FROM A FAMOUS ONE

Judging a wine that you've never drunk before based on its vintage is as a reliable guide to quality as its appellation (see page 67). Both are less important than a producer's resourcefulness and skill. For centuries, it was widely agreed that a 'great' vintage was a warm year that ripened powerful wines with good levels of tannin and alcohol. Something that, due to climate change, now fits many more years than not. On the other hand, an 'off' vintage was one when crops may not have fully ripened, suffered from disease, or rain had diluted at harvest. Yet in spite of those challenges, an accomplished vigneron picking at the right moment and meticulously discarding bad fruit can make an excellent wine that you might enjoy more than one from a more acclaimed harvest.

Vintage reputations are formed by critics at a very early stage, and are prone to contradictions. No one knows how wines will age — not the journalists, merchants, nor the winemakers themselves — and standings are rarely updated. Sure, conditions may have been too hot, too cold, too wet, but great wines can be found in years that have poor reps and vice versa. In 2002 in Brunello di Montalcino, conditions were so dire that the great Gianfranco Soldera said he wasn't going to harvest his vineyards, until his wife Graziella told him that if he didn't do it she'd do it herself. Following his usual uncompromising selection, discarding anything other than ideal berries, he made just 2,000 bottles of wine that consistently ranks among his best. Likewise, 2002 Château Latour, one of the Bordeaux First Growths in a so-called 'off' vintage, is even more delicious than many celebrated years.

To be fair, critics lauded 2002 Latour as the best wine of the vintage. But Bordeaux being Bordeaux, you still can pick it up for around half the price of the more awarded 2000. Indeed, 2002's low yields and good acidity produced a structured, concentrated wine that, like all Latours, should make great old bones. It's still expensive — but on the 'pleasure-to-time-alive ratio' it's a solid investment in future joy (delicious 2011 Latour is also a steal at half the price of the 2010). Over in Burgundy, critics applying the 'warm year = great vintage' criteria have celebrated many overwrought wines that, for my tastes, are not classical styles. I've learnt to avoid many pedestrian 2009 reds from the Côte de Nuits lacking their usual freshness. Counterintuitively, I've always found more to like in white Burgundy — Jean-Marc Roulot's 2009s are stellar across the board, as is Henri Boillot Puligny-Montrachet Premier Cru 'Clos de la Mouchère'.

22

SULPHUR SO GOOD

Or why a little brimstone is not worth a war

Mount Etna-based
winemaker Frank
Cornelissen.

Few phrases in wine-speak are as loaded as 'CONTAINS SULPHITES': two seemingly innocuous words that strike at the heart of righteous *vignerons* on the front lines of the sulphur wars. *Vignerons* who, having never added SO_2 (an often-maligned chemical used widely to inhibit bacteria and prevent oxidation) to their 'natural' *cuvées*, are nevertheless obliged by law to label them with this mark of the beast because all wines contain it as a by-product of fermentation.

I'm not sure why the Natural Wine Police originally identified sulphur as public enemy number one, vilifying it more than toxic farming and the homogenising creep of winery technology—the elements of commercial winemaking most in need of change. Of course, like the food I eat, I want the wine I drink to have had as few interventions and additions as possible. But considering sulphur is the fifth-most abundant element on the planet, occurring naturally not just in vino, but in everything from dried fruit to cauliflower, I never understood the obsession with eliminating it at all costs.

Perhaps the answer lies in the collective psyche and all those parables involving divine retribution by fire and brimstone—ye ancient name for sulphur—entwined in our DNA. Or perhaps it's that clean-living trends coincided with #winefakenews. (Yeah bro, it's the sulphur that gave you a hangover, not the swimming pool of alcohol and umpteen Gauloises.) I've even visited celebrated *vignerons* and witnessed guests ignoring their meticulous farming and superb wines to cast aspersions about whether or not they've added too much sulphur. Talk about myopic. When looking at a beautiful painting, who ignores colour and composition to obsess over the varnish?

Don't get me wrong: *sans soufre* classics such as Gramenon's 1995 'Ceps Centenaires La Mémé' and Emmanuel Houillon-Pierre Overnoy's 2002 Arbois Pupillin Ploussard are among the most soulful wines I've drunk. My problem isn't zero sulphur addition per se, but the dogmatic insistence upon it. A practice that all but such maestros struggle to get right. Charlie Parker once advised jazz heads: "First you learn the instrument, then you learn the music, then you forget all that shit and just play." I only wish more of natural wine's players had received the equivalent memo, and developed an early rigour from which to improvise.

Without pristine fruit, a scrupulously clean cellar, and a clear idea of how to fashion the best wine possible, you don't need to be a master *vigneron* to know that the low-intervention motto "nothing added and nothing taken away" is fiendishly difficult to achieve (or, as Catalonia's Pepe Raventós tells me of making his crystalline Xarel·lo 'De la Vinya del Noguer Alt', "Like climbing a mountain without aid"). Sure, *sans soufre cuvées* can be pure and beautiful, but they're also often unpredictable. Conversely, a tiny amount of sulphur employed at the right moment isn't harmful to humans (unless you're allergic, of course) and can aid a wine's tension and definition, protecting it on its journey from cellar to glass.

But beyond the dogma and flaws routinely presented as signs of authenticity (Diner: "Waiter, my Gamay is corked and re-fermenting." Waiter: "LUCKY YOU!"), there are signs that the brimstone battles are drawing to a close. Indeed, Alice Feiring, long one of natural wine's influential voices, more recently wrote about starting to accept minimal SO_2 additions to counter 'mouse taint', a rank bacterial infection. "I've developed a renewed appreciation for traditional wines, or for me, 'natural enough'. In other words, natural in every way except up to 30ppm of sulphur addition," said Feiring. "I believe that one day drinkers of natural wine will realise that a minimal amount of added sulphur (if needed) isn't the devil. Just as the world shrugged off once trendy, high-octane wines or oaky Chardonnays and the notion that bigger is better, they'll eventually reject this, too."

Bring on such a revitalised appreciation for authentically made wines. Suffering mouse taint — let alone brettanomyces, rampant volatile acidity or oxidation — in pursuit of an ideal is not my idea of fun. Besides, many of natural wine's founders, such as Beaujolais' Marcel Lapierre, routinely rejected substandard batches of their own wines, rather than justify lousiness with intent, as the puritans do. And if insisting on zero sulphur disqualifies many of the world's great wines, from Denis Bachelet to Keller and Coche-Dury, you can count me out. Fortunately, it's not just Feiring who's reappraising their views on minimal SO_2.

Few would have bet that Frank Cornelissen would start using sulphur. Yet the celebrated Sicily-based low-intervention winemaker — both a traditionalist and an iconoclast — has never shirked change. Leaving a career in Antwerp trading classics such as Château Pétrus and Domaine Leflaive to become a *vigneron* on Mount Etna at the beginning of the noughties, he followed his dream of making 'liquid rock ', or, as he says, "the anti-wines, as a reaction to the ever more technological wines being made in the late '90s."

I've followed Cornelissen's Etna project with fascination over the years, although the notion of 'liquid rock' was often more appealing than his crazy

Frank Cornelissen
retrospective,
Harry's Bar,
London.

early vintages. With only the most tenuous relationship to fruit, his wines often seemed to glow Chernobyl pink with tiny suspended fragments of what I mistakenly presumed was lava, like some kind of post-apocalyptic snow globe. Yet after a London tasting of seven vintages of his Munjebel CS 'Chiusa Spagnolo', I came away dazzled by how recent years have become purer and more harmonious through his mastery of details such as harvesting dates, and – the horror – adding minimal SO_2 after racking, when wines are moved from tank to tank. "Starting using sulphur in the 2018 vintage was a big statement because that's a dogma, but it also felt right. Everything needs time," Cornelissen tells me.

Imagine the hand-wringing that must've gone on in natural wine circles when the news broke that he'd also employed Guillaume Thienpont of Pomerol traditionalist Vieux Château Certan as a consultant. But given Cornelissen's classical grounding, it makes total sense. Wanting to understand more about his wines, the duo conducted microbiological analyses. Cornelissen says Thienpont's tasting skills had a profound effect on his own, helping him to focus more on the tactile feeling of well-defined fruit. By introducing tiny levels of SO_2 after racking – rather than at harvest or just before bottling, as is conventional – they've devised a strategy for crunchy deliciousness. "It's an intellectual approach," says Cornelissen.

'Chiusa Spagnolo' is 100% Nerello Mascalese, a dark-skinned Sicilian grape that bears some stylistic similarities to Pinot Noir and Nebbiolo, depending on vintage conditions. While the debut 2012 sailed close to over-ripeness, with a hint of Bovril cube-esque oxidation, the stony-fresh 2013, and opulent 2017, showed Cornelissen beginning to get to grips with the vineyard. However, the 2018 and 2020 wines take purity and precision to a whole new level, with the 2018's delicate perfume reminiscent of

Chambolle-Musigny—albeit with grainier tannins—and the rich, deep and 'liquid-rock'-esque 2020 his most astonishing wine to date. "This is where I wanted to get to years ago!" he coos.

Perhaps, as Cornelissen says, you sometimes have to go beyond the limits to find out where they are. But if this tasting proves anything, it's that a little SO_2 has helped another of his early goals: to demonstrate Etna's different crus. As much as I love the energy of zero-sulphur wines, I wonder if a Burgundian domaine that didn't use any SO_2 in wines from neighbouring crus would find the definition and nuance to be able to discuss 'terroir'. In 2018 Meursault's Jean-Marc Roulot produced an experimental *sans soufre* Aligoté alongside a regular sulphured version. While the regular is linear and precise, the zero-sulphur wine was softer and broader, which, on the evidence of serving it to experienced tasters without telling them what it was, was also less obviously Burgundian. They thought that it was from Jura or the Loire Valley.

Much as such anecdotal tastings suggest to me, a totally inexperienced non-winemaker, that judicious SO_2 addition helps craft sophisticated drinking, I'll resist the demon of generalisations and keep an open mind. Maybe some wines need sulphur to provide a sense of place. But given how some without any at all, from the likes of Jura's François Rousset-Martin, or Loire's Richard Leroy, light up the pleasure receptors in my brain like a chimpanzee on a pinball machine, I'm sometimes inclined not to care. "To make a wine that touches the stars there must be risk," Leroy says. Indeed, his vital, textured Chenin Blancs make me wonder why anyone needs SO_2 at all—until I remember few are as accomplished as he is. Natural wine's great achievements—improving farming and minimising generic winery technology—should be celebrated with gusto. But thank god a few more of us can agree that a little bit of brimstone is not worth a war. ●

Richard Leroy, Rablay-sur-Layon, Anjou, France.

23

CHENIN, CHENIN, CHÉNIN!

Or how dry Chenin Blanc took over the Loire Valley

Nicolas Joly,
Coulée de
Serrant,
Savennières,
Loire Valley.

"Chenin, Chenin, Chenin!" is the rallying cry of New York City sommelier Pascaline Lepeltier, a woman after my own heart. Indeed, I drink just as much, if not more, Loire Valley Chenin Blanc as I do any other white, its dry style growing in popularity over recent years with *vignerons* using organic farming and 'low intervention' winemaking. Chenin Blanc is a non-aromatic 'noble' variety due to its ability to make complex, long-lived wines in a range of styles. Like Chardonnay it soaks up characteristics from the terroir in which it's grown, and has bracing acidity that some drinkers find too intense, but others adore.

Anjou and Savennières have numerous excellent domaines producing dry, textured, invigorating wines such as Thomas Batardière, Domaine aux Moines, Belargus, Benoit Courault, Ferme de la Sansonnière, Mai & Kenji Hodgson, Thibaud Boudignon, Eric Morgat, Richard Leroy and Stéphane Bernaudeau. New-school classics such as Bernaudeau's 'Les Nourrissons' and Leroy's 'Les Noëls de Montbenault' are so packed full of life that if you put them under a microscope you'd surely find a universe of merrily vibrating atoms. "My greatest pleasure is that I don't make wine at all," says Leroy of the simplicity of his methods, using long ferments and élevage to bring equilibrium to his zero-sulphur-addition bottlings. Leroy and fellow *vignerons* Mark Angéli and Jo Pithon first set about proving their Anjou vineyards could produce more than just the sweet wines they were historically famed for around the millennium, and a new tradition was cast.

In Savennières, *vigneronne* Tessa Laroche has taken over the historic Domaine aux Moines with fantastic results. Her 'Roche aux Moines' and young-vine *Vin de France* 'Le Berceau des Fées' are the embodiment of Savennières as Chenin Blanc's most austere and powerful style, with none of the botrytis influence that's often been part of her neighbour Nicolas Joly's Coulée de Serrant wines. Planted in the 1100s by Cistercian monks, Coulée de Serrant old vintages have varied greatly under biodynamics pioneer Joly, the only *vigneron* in Savennières to still use ancient tri selection to pick botrytised grapes. At its best, Coulée de Serrant is a decadent, golden wine with the aromas of everything from candied exotic fruit to bitter marmalade and minerals. Now joined by daughter Virginie, Joly is producing wines that are much drier with less botrytis. They're more consistent, no doubt, but I love the florid eccentricity of wine like his 1996 and 2004. ●

Thomas Batardière
'Les Cocus'
Vin de France
$$$

Mai & Kenji Hodgson
'Les Aussigouins'
Vin de France
$$$

Domaine aux Moines
'Le Berceau des Fées'
Vin de France
$$$

Domaine Belargus
'Treilles'
Anjou
$$$$

Stéphane Bernaudeau
'Les Nourrissons'
Vin de France
$$$$

Nicolas Joly
'Clos de la Coulée de Serrant'
AOC Coulée de Serrant, Monopole
$$$$

Richard Leroy
'Les Noëls de Montbenault'
Vin de France
$$$$

24

CHÂTEAU-GRILLET

The highs and lows of France's most enigmatic white wine

One of my favourite volumes of the 1970s children's book series *Barbapapa* features the family of colourful polymorphous blobs living in utopian bliss until a gang of angry construction vehicles arrives to spoil the party. Which is kind of what happened to the owners of Château-Grillet — arguably France's most paradisiacal vineyard and enigmatic white wine — at the beginning of the same decade, when chemical company ICI built a smoke-billowing factory a cork's throw across the River Rhône. Indeed, the Rhône Valley, which runs from just below Lyon towards the south coast, is notorious for its contrast of the idyllic and the industrial, a legacy of the post-war push for growth. Yet given Château-Grillet's iconic wisteria-covered stone walls and terraced amphitheatre of Viognier, one might have hoped that even La République's work-dodging bureaucrats could have found somewhere else — anywhere else — to bugger up the view instead.

Château-Grillet has long been a mythical wine, even if it has often fallen short of the quality a mythical wine should achieve. It's certainly not instantly obvious how it forged such a reputation. For a start, there are no superstar mature vintages available to pass on the flame. No equivalent of the liquid cashmere Cheval Blanc 1990, or Coche-Dury's interstellar 1996s to ignite new passions. Grillets that are said to be notable were made in such small quantities — 1,000 bottles of the 1961, for example — that there was never enough to develop vintage ratings. It's frankly a wonder the domaine commercially exists today. And whereas legends tend to galvanise around game-changing visionaries such as Burgundy's Henri Jayer, or mavericks such as Jacques Reynaud — whose topsy-turvy cellar

produces the spellbinding Château Rayas — the low-key Neyret-Gachet family's near 200-year custodianship of Château-Grillet produced highly variable results. So, what's all the fuss about?

AOC Château-Grillet is among France's smallest appellations, owned by one domaine (also called Château-Grillet), farming one grape (Viognier) to produce one flagship wine (you guessed it, Château-Grillet, now alongside a Côtes du Rhône Blanc and a Condrieu). Located beneath the village of St Michel-sur-Rhône, a one-hour drive south-west of Lyon airport, it is bordered by the much larger, also exclusively Viognier-based appellation of Condrieu, which during the 1960s was so poor that it teetered on the brink of extinction. The immediate surroundings have few, if any, noble buildings of note, and it's easy to imagine generations of people looking up at Château-Grillet's fairy-tale towers high on the hillside, and viscerally feeling themselves in the presence of majesty. Certainly, the first time I saw a photo of Château-Grillet, in a random wine book one grotty afternoon in west London, I felt the same thing.

In the late 18th century, Thomas Jefferson developed enough of a taste for Grillet to pay it a visit, while in the 1920s Curnonsky rated it the third-best white in the world. "Of all the wines made from the Viognier around Condrieu, the palm must go to a very great, exceptional, marvellous and suave white wine: the most rare Château-Grillet, a golden and flamboyant wine cultivated in a vineyard of less than five acres, a wine above commercialisation, just about untraceable and jealously guarded by its one owner," wrote Curnonsky. He went on to describe it as "lively, violent, changeable like a pretty woman, with a flavour of the flowers of vines and almonds, and a stunning bouquet of wild flowers and violets" — it's unclear whether the Grillet he wrote of was made in a sweet style, or dry as it is today. Curnonsky also mentions the wine reaching 15% ABV, an undoubted luxury during an era when grapes often struggled to ripen.

More evidence of Grillet greatness is found in Maurice Healy's 1940 classic *Stay Me with Flagons*. Comparing the "pebbly taste" of a 75-year-old bottle of 1861 Château-Grillet to Chablis, he goes on to say that it had "a majesty greater than that attained by Chablis, or any Burgundy except Montrachet." Of course, many legendary wines find themselves compared to Côte d'Or royalty and praised for their ageability. But Grillet's extreme inaccessibility undoubtedly made it even more enigmatic (the domaine still only accepts a handful of visits each year). "I was conscious of the awe that surrounded the estate," said Rhône expert John Livingstone-Learmonth of being granted access in 1973. "This was justifiable, because there had been some 1960s Grillets of great authority and class — the 1969 'Cuvée Renaissance' and the 1966 spring to mind. The Neyret-Gachet family also kept a very low profile, so little was known about the inner workings." Likewise, my only visit to Château-Grillet, in 2016, was a special, if slightly surreal, experience, with its Lilliputian dimensions lending it the air of an oversized doll's house and garden.

Perhaps legendary wines, like heroes, are better left unmet. But that doesn't stop one wondering what magic — or, often more realistically, what malfunction — lies under such venerated corks. So, having bought one of the 1,730 bottles Château-Grillet made of 1969 'Cuvée Renaissance' (a selection of top barrels), I opened an over half-century-old Viognier — with low expectations. As a rule, Viognier is best drunk between three and eight

years of harvest, one of the few fine wines that doesn't benefit from ageing (Grillet and great years of Georges Vernay Condrieu 'Coteau de Vernon' are notable exceptions). As with certain friends, very old wine requires you to make rather too many excuses for the merciless effect of oxygen and time. But this amber-coloured 1969 improved in the glass over an hour—a perfume of ripe apricots, orange pith, caramel and spice suggesting sweetness but instead contrasting with a bone-dry, austere, chalky finish. Having also drunk surprisingly youthful—though not quite as impressive—mature bottles of Grillet 1974 and 1989, here was affirmation that this mythical terroir can grow complex, long-lived wines.

In 2011, the Neyret-Gachet family sold Château-Grillet to François Pinault's Artémis Domaines after almost two centuries of ownership, heralding a new era of ambition that has brought much more consistency. Buying the estate certainly cannot have been a commercial decision, with annual production still in the low thousands. But for a wine lover such as Frédéric Engerer (who, 20 years ago, was hired fresh out of business school by Pinault to run the venerable Château Latour—an appointment that shocked the Bordelais establishment due to his relative lack of experience) the chance to take custodianship of such a legendary terroir, and push it to its full potential, proved irresistible. Besides renovating the winery and converting the vineyards to biodynamics, one of his most important decisions was parting ways with Neyret-Gachet consultant Denis Dubourdieu, professor of oenology at Bordeaux University and a revered 'wine scientist'. When Engerer sought a second opinion on harvesting from *vigneron* Jean-Louis Chave, he was advised to wait ten days more than Dubourdieu had suggested, resulting in riper grapes. Bringing in a fresh team, a new direction was cast.

Of course, I'm a sucker for a good myth, even if the myth of Château-Grillet has for the most part been a bit more delicious than the reality. So, when in May 2022 Engerer hosted a small tasting at Noble Rot Soho of every vintage he has produced since taking charge, it was satisfying to find more substance around the estate's dusty old bones. Dry white wines with extraordinary textural richness and finesse, from their inaugural 2011 to the nascent 2020, all had enough weight to pair as well with heavier red-meat dishes as the chicken and morels we ate alongside (although in its most successful years Grillet is a much tenser, linear wine than the blowsy, oaked 'prestige' Condrieu *cuvées* to which it's sometimes compared). Sure, it is a resolutely off-trend white Rhône, the qualities of which need discerning with a different mindset to the lithe, high-acidity white wines now in vogue. But why should anyone visiting The National Gallery not be able to appreciate the greatness of both Rembrandt and Bridget Riley on their own, very different, terms?

Among my favourites, 2014 Château-Grillet smelt like fresh-from-the-oven *canelés* and honeysuckle: a refined wine with layers of gunflint, nuts and mango—the latter being the main giveaway that you're not drinking top Grand Cru Burgundy. Likewise, the saline and direct 2013—the grippy chalky atoms of which I pictured forming the shape of an arrow on my tongue—and the exuberant, stony-floral-spice-scented 2019, finishing refreshingly bitter and long. Every sip delivered a little high. Of course, a cynic might gripe at technical know-how eradicating characterful edges, as at some other historic old-school domaines. But as the edges of so many pre-2011 vintages of Grillet were never very desirable, why sweat the upgrade? Perhaps, unlike Maurice Healy, I would not go quite as far as describing 1969 Château-Grillet 'Cuvée Renaissance' as 'magisterial'. But will future generations of winos rave about these younger vintages in decades to come? Why the hell not? As a wise man once said, when the legend becomes fact—print the legend. ●

25

THE VINOUS EQUIVALENT OF A FEEL-GOOD ROMANTIC COMEDY

Chewing over Condrieu, Northern Rhône Valley, France

Chéry vineyard,
Condrieu,
Northern Rhône
Valley, France.

As wine labels go, E Guigal Condrieu 'La Doriane' is a retiring little number. Resplendent with gold foil and a kitsch illustration of spring blossoms, it encapsulates why many winos consider this aromatic Northern Rhône white wine appellation passé. "What is there to love about the smells of an exotic flower shop that has been closed up without air conditioning for too long?" asked writer Alice Feiring of Viognier, the grape Condrieu is made from. With many overwrought renditions, not least 'La Doriane', I feel her pain. But although my favourite Condrieus from Domaines Vernay, André Perret and François Dumas offer more restrained perfumes of apricots, passion fruits and honeysuckles, for me it's the salty-bitter aftertaste from the soils they're grown on that sets them apart. Contrasting custard-cream texture with bitter-quinine finishes, I'd go all in for such gourmand white wines.

Fessing up to being a Condrieu aficionado may be as hip as admitting you're a closet Richard Curtis super-fan, but these wines deserve just as much respect as neighbouring AOC Côte-Rôtie's superstar Syrahs and other Northern Rhône royalty. Viognier is planted around the world, but nothing compares to that which is grown on AOC Condrieu's 200ha of steep terraced vineyards, and the *monopole* enclave AOC Château-Grillet (see previous chapter). Further south in the Languedoc, commercial wineries farm big yields on flat lands producing thin wines missing their mouthwatering bitterness.

I like drinking sumptuous Condrieu at the beginning of a meal, although it's a happy companion to other southern pleasures such as black truffles

on scrambled eggs, or chicken liver terrine spread thick on warm buttered toast. And if, as old-school *vignerons* say, terroir can be felt in a wine's texture more than its aromas, here's the evidence. Great Condrieu tastes like it's literally been infused with its unique arzelle topsoil — a type of decomposed granite mica schist — compensating for Viognier's moderate natural acidity. One of the growers' biggest challenges is choosing the right time to harvest Viognier, a capricious grape that loves low yields and high elevations, which help assuage its tendency to spike rapidly in ripeness. In warm vintages an extra two days on the vines before picking can add 1.5% ABV more to wines that routinely attain 15% ABV. And if growers go too early, under-ripe Viognier is a whole other flavour of hell.

Unusually for a 'fine wine', Condrieu is not one to age: I'm happy buying ad-hoc bottles and revelling in their youthful exuberance, its perennial unfashionability making it unlikely that prices will spiral. While 1990 Georges Vernay Condrieu 'Coteau de Vernon' — a wine I would've sworn was 30 years younger if I hadn't seen the label — disproved the general view that Viognier can't age, it's a rare exception. Comparing 2010 Vernay 'Les Terrasses de l'Empire' to the 2018 version, the older wine was much darker with less tension, whereas the younger was more energetic with the vivid flavours of pear, rotting passion fruit and custard tart. Whether 'Les Terrasses', 'Coteau de Vernon', or the magnificently titled 'Les Chaillées de l'Enfer' ('the gates of hell') — Vernay is Condrieu's benchmark address.

Christine Vernay and husband Paul Amsellem took over the domaine in 1997 from her late father Georges, a man who saved Condrieu from the abyss. During the decades following the Second World War there was little interest in the now globally renowned Northern Rhône, where steep terraces make the use of labour-saving mechanised equipment impossible. Seeing no commercial way forward, scores of growers sold up — if they could find buyers for their land — taking jobs in new industries opening around the region, in what became nicknamed 'Chemical Valley'. In 1965, only 8ha of Viognier vines remained on the planet — all of which were in Condrieu.

"We didn't think things were bad at the time because my father didn't make a big deal out of it," says Christine of when Georges, and Étienne Guigal, founder of Guigal wines, were the two main growers still promoting the appellation. Étienne subsidised his Condrieu and Côte-Rôtie sales with mass-market Southern Rhône wines, and his son Marcel continued buying and marketing many small growers' wines — at one point selling half of all wine made within the appellation. But it wasn't until the mid-'80s that interest in Condrieu picked up and passionate foreign winemakers, such as California's Josh Jensen, began planting Viognier elsewhere in the world.

Guigal's entry-level *cuvée* was the first Condrieu I ever drank. Time seemed to slow and the wine expanded into a three-dimensional bubble. Since then my taste has evolved, and while I appreciate the pop appeal of its sibling 'La Doriane', I find more overwrought years too much. I was also disappointed re-tasting a ten-year-old Yves Cuilleron 'Vertige', which spends 18 months in new oak, and was already past its best, although his liquorice-cream 'Vernon', and Vignobles Levet's Condrieu are both superb. Elsewhere, François Dumas uses long macerations and minimal sulphur to make a unique, pared-back natural style, and André Perret 'Coteau de Chéry' is a heady cocktail of apricot, minerals and cream that never fails to do the business. Little wonder then that when in the third century the Roman Emperor Probus signed a decree to uproot half of Gaul's vines to stem overproduction, he exempted this 'darling hillside'. ●

A SHORTCUT TO DRINKING GREAT CONDRIEU

CHEWING THE FAT
OTHER TEXTURAL GREATS YOU NEED TO KNOW

Domaine Georges Vernay
Condrieu 'Coteau de Vernon'
$$$$

Domaine Georges Vernay
Condrieu 'Les Chaillées de l'Enfer'
$$$

Domaine André Perret
Condrieu 'Coteau de Chéry'
$$$

Domaine François Dumas
Condrieu
$$$

Domaine Jamet
Condrieu 'Vernillon'
$$$

López de Heredia Blanco
Rioja Blanco
Rioja, Spain
$$$-$$$$

López de Heredia's Haro cellars are straight out of a fairy tale, a moody underworld covered in mould. Now run by the fourth generation of the family, it held onto its traditional ethos during the '80s and '90s, a time when many Rioja bodegas lost their characters due to the rise of winery technology, and remains unchanged to this day. 'Viña Bosconia' and 'Viña Tondonia' are López de Heredia's flagship cuvées, produced as reds and rare white blends of Viura and Malvasia with long American oak barrel-ageing. "We used to receive congratulations from all over the world for our white, but it was like Sherry — everybody said how marvellous it was but hardly anyone drinks it," says María José López de Heredia. "We had so much stock of it that we reduced the amount we produced. Now everyone wants to buy old vintages and we don't have any to sell." The white Rioja is a thick, full-bodied gastronomic gem with distinctive aromas of beeswax, orange pith and brown sugar.

Joško Gravner takes delivery
of Georgian qvevri in Oslavia,
Friuli, 2004.

Gravner
Ribolla Gialla
Friuli, Italy
$$$-$$$$

Joško Gravner was one of modern
Italy's most celebrated vignerons
until a moment of clarity made him
change his life. Returning from a
trip to California disillusioned by
how so many of the wines tasted the
same, he stripped his Friuli winery
of technology and reinstalled a
mechanical basket press and large old
oak casks in search of a traditional
style. In 1996 hail obliterated his
crops so he experimented on whatever
grapes he could salvage with long
macerations on the skins, and fell
in love with the results. Next, his
quest for authenticity took him to
Georgia in search of large earthenware
amphorae, and after teething problems
selling his new amber/orange wines to
regular customers without warning them
about the changes ("They thought I was
crazy"), they are now the benchmark
for the style. Soaking up Ribolla
Gialla tannins over five months of
fermentation on the skins in Georgian
clay qvevris, followed by a further
six months ageing in qvevris and six
years in large oak barrels, these are
textural, complex wines that should be
served at cellar temperature rather
than chilled. "It's life itself that I
try to put into wines," says Gravner.
"You don't create wine by adding
additives, you help it to be what
it is."

26

BIG SMOKE

*One of the most mouth-watering
wine trends of recent years*

The Côte Blonde,
southern slopes
of Côte-Rôtie,
Northern Rhône
Valley, France.

Smoke everywhere. Smoke scenting everything from eel to ice cream on the wood grill at the Basque Country's Asador Etxebarri; smoke perfuming slow-cooked, gelatinous turbot at London's Brat. Smoke above the backyards of countless wannabe BBQ pit-masters; smoke curing the catch of the day in Secret Smokehouse's railway arch. I'd bet my last euro that smoked food has never fallen out of fashion since man discovered fire 500,000 years ago — just as I'd wager that there's no chance of the rise in popularity of smoky-delicious wines slowing any time soon. Take Renaud Boyer 2018 Puligny-Montrachet 'Les Reuchaux' for example: beyond its moreish deliciousness what I found most remarkable about it was how much it tasted like Frazzles, the stupendously smoky bacon crisps of yore.

Never mind the recent trends for 'orange', '#natty' or 'icon' wines: 'smoky wine' is a thing, and I love it. Of course, by that I don't mean wines from vineyards tainted by forest fires, but beautifully crafted reds and whites where smokiness evokes a feeling of familiarity. Indeed, if great vino has the power to transport you to another place and time, why not revel in being made to feel like a crisp-munching kid at the back of the school bus again? Such aromas and flavours come as a result of toasted oak barrels, soils, and/or a process called 'reduction'. Besides the aforementioned porkiness, if you're a white Burgundy lover who's been fortunate enough to drink old vintages of Coche-Dury and Leflaive, you might recognise this as the fuzzy whiff of an extinguished match framing immaculate hazelnut lemon-cream flavours. I adore how this accentuates other non-fruit elements, bolstering definition in the wines.

Today most wines are made by reductive winemaking (fastidiously 'topping-up' wine ageing in oak barrels or using temperature-controlled steel tanks to minimise exposure to oxygen) — although there's a big difference between the 'good' and 'bad' kind, where wines become so starved of oxygen they start smelling of bad eggs. But besides reductive winemaking, and top domaines' unique recipes for oak ageing, smokiness in wine is influenced by soils. At Stéphane Tissot's winery in Arbois, Jura, he demonstrates the flavours that dark trias clay imparts to his wines while hosting a tasting. "Which soil do you think this was grown on?" he'll ask of two unidentified, tangy-saline Chardonnays. The wines grown on clay-dominated soils always have a smokiness that those from limestone simply do not.

But, for me, nowhere on the planet does smoky wine quite like the Northern Rhône Valley. Consult old wine texts about Côte-Rôtie and, again, you find 'smoky bacon' as one of the most typical descriptors used for its benchmark Syrah. To the best of my knowledge no pigs have ever been harmed as part of the winemaking process at any of the local domaines (although, hey, who knows — it is southern France), but there's no denying the porky revelation of drinking Domaine Jamet Côte-Rôtie. Mighty Noël Verset Cornas, one of the Northern Rhône's all-time greats, brings me back to the same old question: how can such an animalistic, wild, smoky evocation of a landscape be made just from grapes? And drunk alongside a charred rib of dairy cow at Asador Etxebarri, or a lamb chop at Brat? Lord, if you're going to take me, take me now. ●

Domaine Tissot
Arbois 'Les Bruyères'
Chardonnay
$$$

Domaine Guiberteau
Saumur 'Brézé'
$$$

Domaine Jamet
Côte-Rôtie
$$$$

Domaine Noël Verset
Cornas
$$$$

Domaine Coche-Dury
Meursault (especially pre-2013)
$$$$-$$$$$

Domaine Jamet Côte-Rôtie, and rare
single-vineyard Côte-Brune (above),
have signature smoky aromas.

27

SAINTED LOVE

Building legacies in St-Joseph, Northern Rhône Valley, France

Jean-Louis Chave
in Clos Florentin
vineyard, St-
Joseph, Northern
Rhône Valley,
France.

After more than my fair share of visits to vineyards, you'll forgive me for saying that many of them blur into one. Yet more unfathomably old soils; yet more common trellising-systems; yet another moment of despair when cornered by a *vigneron* who—jabbering away about 'pruning structures'—can't read their audience. But every so often, I stand among the dust and the vines of a hillside like St-Joseph 'Les Chalaix', astonished by its scale—and the bloody-mindedness of Jean-Louis Chave, who prised it back from the forest—and I think: This is glorious.

Seeing 'Les Chalaix' for the first time was, quite literally, breathtaking: the solar-powered monument to Syrah made me surrender my last lungful like a goldfish that had leapt out of its bowl. I don't think Chave, who was standing next to me at the time, noticed. Nor did he seem to notice the amazement that overwhelmed me as the magnitude of what he's achieved over the past couple of decades in St-Joseph dawned. Because 'Les Chalaix' has 'LEGACY' written all over it—and with his restoration of 14ha of uncommonly steep vineyards, abandoned since phylloxera in the 1860s, this one will last for centuries.

In 1992, Jean-Louis took over his family domaine and started renovating St-Joseph 'Bachasson'—a site once owned by his ancestors. At first his father Gérard wondered why he didn't just focus on their Hermitage. Both red and white Chave Hermitage rank among the world's greatest wines—savorous pure Syrahs and gourmand Marsanne/Roussanne blends that are the stuff of winos' dreams. But Chave Jr isn't one to sit back. With it near-impossible to buy more land on Hermitage, it seemed obvious to him to reclaim the neighbouring homelands with which it has long had a symbiotic relationship – St-Joseph's humble yin to Hermitage's noble yang.

In 1999, Chave started piecing together 'Les Chalaix', buying ten plots from different owners. "'Les Chalaix' was a big construction project, like Hermitage was centuries ago," he says. The similarities are obvious. Like Saar's colossal Scharzhofberger, or Chablis' Grands Crus, these vineyards feel alive. Later in the day, we see workmen building terraces on the gigantic granite hillside next door to 'Bachasson'. "I don't know if they know how much work it is… yet," says Chave, wiping his brow in the summer heat.

If Hermitage is straightforward to define – a 137ha hill once owned by the church and nobility who sold it to peasants after phylloxera – sprawling St-Joseph is not. Originally based around five valleys – 'Les Chalaix', 'Bachasson', 'Ste-Épine', 'La Dardouille' and 'St-Joseph' itself – the appellation was established in 1956, stretching 30 miles along the right bank of the Rhône from Chavanay in the north to Châteaubourg in the south. Yet due to AOC St-Joseph's rapid expansion of 30ha or more every year – more than doubling in size from 600ha in the early '90s to over 1,400ha today – only a small percentage of wines are exciting.

"We've terroir every bit as good as Cornas and Côte-Rôtie but people are planting in the wrong places – because it's easier," says Jean Gonon as our feet sink into the Ste-Épine 'Aubert' decomposed gneiss, very much one of the right places. Gonon bought the vineyard from the revered late *vigneron* Raymond Trollat, occasionally bottling the fruit of its 100-year-old vines as a rare 'Vieilles Vignes' *cuvée*, but more frequently vinifying it as the spine of his standard St-Joseph *cuvée*, one of southern France's best-loved reds.

Jean and his brother Pierre took over Domaine Pierre Gonon in 1988 and have gradually elevated it from being a provider of rustic house wines to local bistros to world-acclaimed growers of fine-scented gems. I adore Gonon's smoky, floral fragrances that, perhaps more than any other reds I know, instantly conjure the feeling of blustery autumn weather, and could only originate here in the Northern Rhône. Like all who farm grapes in St-Joseph, where everything must be done by hand, the Gonons are true *vignerons*. In nearby Crozes-Hermitage one person can farm 15ha of vines by using machinery and irrigation, but here it takes one person for a single hectare.

Raymond Trollat died in 2023 at the age of 91 and has become a patron saint of Syrah. AOC St-Joseph had suffered a previous huge loss when its godfather, Jean-Louis Grippat, sold his domaine to Guigal in 2001. From a bloodline of growers, Grippat's father died young, leaving the family to sell grapes to the *négociant* Chapoutier. But a couple of weeks before the poor 1963 harvest, Chapoutier declined to take its crops, leaving it facing disaster. Fortunately, Jaboulet – producer of legendary Hermitage 'La Chapelle' – stepped in, offering advice and barrels, and so Grippat started making wine. More progressive than the resolutely untechnological Trollat, Grippat also owned the appellation's top vineyards, 'Vignes de l'Hospice' and *lieu-dit* 'St-Joseph' – Grands Crus in all but name. His 1991 St-Joseph – whose sublime fragrance I'd happily dab behind my ears – could go nose-to-nose with a top Hermitage.

Today, Grippat is often seen riding his bike around the vineyards. He also offers support to his nephew Julien Cécillon and wife Nancy

Jean Gonon, Domaine Pierre Gonon, Mauves, Northern Rhône Valley.

Overleaf: Jean-Louis Chave in St-Joseph 'Les Chalaix'.

Kerschen, makers of an excellent St-Joseph called 'Babylone'. "I never liked the heavy style of local wines that were around when I was growing up in St-Joseph," says Cécillon. "We called them 'three hand wines' — one hand to hold the glass and two to hold the table." Part of a generation embracing much-improved, often organic farming that also includes Hervé Souhaut and La Ferme des Sept Lunes, the couple started their domaine from scratch and will soon expand their St-Joseph holdings. "The last time we planted a vineyard, Jean-Louis Chave came to help us plan where to put the rows," says Julien. "He looked around and said, 'Easy, this'll take two minutes.'"

Chave is the man to help sow the new seeds of St-Joseph, for sure, but when he tells me that he doesn't know if he believes in it as an appellation, he only believes in specific places, it's clear what he means. His *monopole* 'Clos Florentin' is the last vineyard I visit — although at first, I'm not sure I believe in this 'specific place'. The Northern Rhône is nicknamed 'Chemical Valley' because of its abundance of heavy industry so when, from high up on 'Les Chalaix', Chave points out some flatlands next to an industrial unit in the distance, I wonder if I am missing something. How wrong could I be? The undulating 'Clos Florentin' is a garden-paradise, with centenarian vines, flowers, wildlife, ponds — and even its own Belle Époque-era folly. Bought in 2009 from the long-organic Domaine Florentin, it produces the first of what Chave hopes will be several characterful single-vineyard bottlings. "I want to give back to history what history gave to me," says Chave, as we sit in the shade of a tree and take in the surroundings. "It's all been possible because of Hermitage." ●

Domaine Pierre Gonon
St-Joseph
$$$-$$$$

Domaine Romaneaux-Destezet
(Hervé Souhaut)
St-Joseph 'Ste Épine'
$$$

Domaine Julien Cécillon
St-Joseph 'Babylone'
$$$

Domaine Jean-Louis Chave
St-Joseph 'Clos Florentin'
$$$$

Domaine Raymond Trollat
St-Joseph
$$$$$

Julien Cécillon and Nancy Kerschen,
Domaine Julien Cécillon, St-Joseph.

28

PEAKY VINERS

On the slopes of Savoie, France's newest fine wine frontier

Learning to ski was not a high point of my youth. On my first day in the French Alps in 1989 a sociopathic skiing instructor, citing my lousy balance, insisted on taking me down a black run "so you can see what it's like". "What it's like" was a formative experience—as was an abortive attempt to buy a lift pass from an immoveable ticket clerk using my nascent foreign-language skills. Neither exactly fostered a connection to Alpine culture. Decades on, rambling across Le Feu—one of Savoie's steepest vineyards—with winemaker and owner of ZigZag ski school Adrien Vallier, I wonder whether, if I'd enrolled with him, I could've made a fluent downhiller. But I'm not here for winter sports. I've returned after all these years in search of quality Savoyard vino—something that's so much easier to find now than back then.

Ask pals if they like Savoie wine and chances are they won't be able to tell you. For the most part, fine-wine production here has only existed for a couple of decades. "People used to say that in a good year you could use Savoie wines to clean your windows, but in a bad it'd scratch them," says Vallier, before bursting into laughter. The wines were tart, often sugary fodder designed to wash down the local resorts' après-ski fondues and raclettes—quality here was never as important as quantity. Yet, slowly, a revolution began. Vallier's forebears reimagined Savoie wine by tempering its intrinsic high-altitude freshness with more depth and body. From red Mondeuse grandmasters Michel Grisard and Jacques Maillet to Bergeron (a.k.a. Roussanne) maestro Gilles Berlioz, and the much-missed Dominique Belluard—who, after years elevating Ayze's rare Gringet, tragically died in 2020 — its idiosyncratic styles have many different things to say.

Savoie might be the most spectacular wine region on the planet: a sparsely populated part of eastern France that, due largely to these lesser-known grapes and customs, is sometimes erroneously compared to Jura. But unlike Jura — the west-facing hills of which were separated from Burgundy's east-facing Côte d'Or millions of years ago and sit around the same level — Savoie is mountainous, full of gargantuan peaks and high-altitude pastures. Looking at Mont Blanc from Le Feu, near Chamonix on one of the main ski-tourism routes, I consider how radical it was of Belluard to transform the reputation of Gringet from Savoyard oddity into an adored cult white wine. He was also almost the only *vigneron* to make this rustic grape — which only grows in this particular part of France — as a still wine as well as a traditional sparkling. His crystalline 'Le Feu' and 'Les Alpes' *cuvées* are full of unique, stony-citrus-herbal Alpine flavours.

Back in Ayze today, Adrien Vallier's sliding-doors moment came when acclaimed Burgundian Vincent Dureuil enrolled at ZigZag ski school. Dureuil-Janthial Rullys have long been insiders' tips, and after Vincent invited Vallier to work the harvest in the Côte Chalonnaise, the pair began trading ski lessons for winemaking ones. In 2018 Domaine Vallier was born, producing a worthy successor to Belluard. We drink his first four vintages of Gringet on plastic garden furniture high on a drizzly Le Feu while eating veal chops. I recall André Jullien's words in *Topographie de tous les vignobles connus* (1832) about the grape: "[Gringet] has the unique property of not causing inebriation so long as one does not leave the table; but as soon as one takes the fresh air, one loses the use of one's legs, and one is forced to sit down."

Yet Savoie is a wet region with a short growing season between spring thaw and autumn freeze, so grapes are often harvested at low sugar levels only capable of producing low alcohol. Given two centuries ago our climate was cooler, what was it that incapacitated Jullien? Some kind of Gringet moonshine? As the planet warms, it'll become harder to find compelling wines such as Vallier's with moderate ABVs. But you still need to choose Savoie bottles carefully to avoid those with a lack of intensity, often made by growers who consider chaptalisation (adding sugar to extend fermentations, creating more alcohol) a mortal sin. Perhaps they might consider learning from the pioneering Michel Grisard, who helped put the region on the map: he not only restricted yields and did away with farming chemicals and commercial yeasts to make world-class Mondeuse, but chaptalised nearly every vintage so it reached a balanced 12% ABV.

Grisard's 2002 Domaine Prieuré St Christophe 'Mondeuse Cuvée Prestige', drunk at two decades old, is proof of top Savoie wine's potential for graceful longevity — one of the qualities that sets 'fine' wines apart. As soon as it was poured, I pictured its pronounced smoky-mulchy red- and black-currant aromas floating across the dining room like a *Looney Tunes* perfume cloud, revealing Mondeuse Noire's ancestral relationship with Syrah as clearly as some of the steepest parts of the local vineyards recall the slopes of the Northern Rhône. Grisard's legacy lives on in his rare Domaine Prieuré St Christophe bottles, which are now highly sought after — with prices to match. But it's also embodied in far more accessible form at Domaine des Ardoisières, another Savoie winery he set up with current

Brice Omont, Domaine des Ardoisières, Savoie. Domaine des Ardoisières' winery is overlooked by the imposing Fortress of Miolans, a former prison where, in 1772, the Marquis de Sade was incarcerated.

winemaking incumbent Brice Omont, and among the most exciting domaines in France.

Grisard and Omont's aim was to make wines that were different as well as demonstrably Savoie and, as with any project prioritising dreams over profits, they made the style of wines they love to drink themselves. Omont, originally from Champagne, adored Burgundy, as well as Didier Dagueneau's game-changing Loire Valley whites, the region where he initially planned to make wine. But following a chance meeting in 2003, Grisard convinced him to move up into the mountains to help restore the terraces of more than 400 rented plots around the village of Cevins. Grisard retired in 2010, leaving Domaine des Ardoisières, which includes slopes as steep as Côte-Rôtie, to Omont's stewardship. I adore his white 2022 'Argile Blanc' – a linear, arrow-shaped blend of Jacquère (Savoie's most planted grape), Chardonnay and Mondeuse Blanche – and his Pinot-esque red 2020 'Améthyste', an equal-parts blend of Mondeuse Noire and Persan that smells of rose and Alpine herbs. These are among the best quality-to-price ratio 'fine' wines available today.

Famed for snow sports, especially following the 1992 Winter Olympics in Albertville, Savoyard land is expensive to buy. Which is why the Cevins project, and Les Vignes de Paradis – another of my favourite domaines – have had to find creative ways to succeed. Indeed, the traffic-choked town of Douvaine near Lake Geneva isn't an obvious place to begin cultivating interstellar vino. Instead of Gringet or Mondeuse, here the spotlight particularly falls on Chasselas (nearby Switzerland's most planted white grape, see page 55), which *vigneron* Dominique Lucas crafts in an array of extraordinarily rich and mineral expressions. Originally from Burgundy, Lucas grew disillusioned with his homeland's attitudes to chemical farming and land costs. In 2001 he took a job in Haute-Savoie, and after gradually buying up plots of old-vine Chasselas as well as planting other varieties he became one of very few artisanal winemakers in the area.

Frankly, the appellations of Crépy, Marin, Marignan and Ripaille, where Lucas's vines are located (but rarely classified as such), are as revered for their fine wines as London is for its palm-fringed beaches. But by adopting cutting-edge farming techniques and harvesting low yields of late-picked fruit with multiple passes through the vineyards, there's no question of Lucas's wines needing chaptalisation. Inside his winery, an array of different methods and vessels are employed, including a concrete replica of the Great Pyramid of Giza (of course) used for a Chardonnay called 'Kheops', and a wonderful umami-laden Chasselas aged under a veil of *flor*, 'Vin des Allobroges' *sous voile*. In a slightly more orthodox style, 2019 Chasselas 'C de Marin' is a tropical, floral, salty honey-bomb of a white wine so full of material you can see it suspended in the bright golden juice – the antithesis of numerous generic Swiss Chasselas that struggle to reach 11.5% ABV. Truly, Les Vignes de Paradis is a gloriously off-piste project for this lackadaisical sub-region. ●

Domaine Les Vignes de Paradis
'C de Marin' Chasselas
Vin des Allobroges
$$$

Domaine des Ardoisières
'Améthyste'
Vin des Allobroges
$$$

Domaine Belluard
'Le Feu' Gringet
Vin de Savoie
$$$

Domaine Prieuré St Christophe
'Mondeuse Tradition'
Vin des Allobroges
$$$$

Domaine Vallier
'Cépage Gringet'
Vin de Savoie
$$$

Dominique Lucas, Vignes de
Paradis, Savoie.

29

PUSH IT TO THE LIMIT

Reimagining Priorat, Catalonia, Spain

Priorat
vineyards,
Catalonia, Spain.

After "fancy some Blue Nun?" the most improbable proposition you might hear in a modern British wine bar has to be "fancy a bottle of Priorat?" For this mountainous Spanish wine region is one of the country's least fashionable, with a reputation so cold that penguins could colonise its spectacularly steep slopes (if its climate wasn't so hot, that is). Indeed, when I told a pal that I was travelling to Priorat to discover more about its powerful reds and lesser-spotted whites, they looked at me like I'd confused a Big Mac for haute cuisine. Yet if I've only learnt one thing over the past decade from visiting vineyards, it's that everywhere has a story. And Priorat's has a Grand Canyon-sized chasm between elegant wines that I love – and overwrought booze-bombs I definitely do not.

Priorat vies with Ribeira Sacra and the Mosel Valley as the most challenging – some might say stupid – place I've witnessed people farming grapes. But these hellish-to-work hillsides offer vines good sunlight exposure and drainage, and once you've tasted wines from local producers such as Terroir al Límit and Família Nin-Ortiz the suffering becomes more understandable. Priorat is an isolated area of extraordinary beauty west of Barcelona, based around 12 medieval villages and the abandoned monastery of Cartoixa. The monastery dates back to 1193, when folklore says that a delegation of visiting French clergymen met a shepherd who told them he'd had a vision of angels on a stairway in the sky. Whether the sheep botherer had an appetite for psilocybin mushrooms remains unclear. Nonetheless, the clergymen founded Cartoixa and the town of Scala Dei ('God's Stairway') the following year.

Monks made wine in Priorat for centuries, until in 1835 Spain's Prime Minister Juan Álvarez Mendizábal began confiscating swathes of ecclesiastical properties. Few church buildings survived, and a decade later Cartoixa and its vineyards were sold to a syndicate of families. When in the 1880s phylloxera decimated European viticulture, many inhabitants left in search of a more prosperous living, a trend later exacerbated by the Spanish Civil War. But you can't keep a good mystic-monastical vineyard region down, and in 1974 Cellers de Scala Dei was re-founded in parts of the monastery, making the first contemporary Priorat wine.

When I visited Cellers de Scala Dei, winemaker Ricard Rofes opened a bottle of its debut 1974, which had sadly seen better days, but also a deep crimson 1975 with lively acidity and a fine sandy texture that demonstrated the wines' potential for long ageing. Grown in Priorat's highest, most northerly vineyards, and fermented whole bunch with gentle extraction, its Garnacha and Cariñena blends are not what many wine lovers think of when they think of Priorat reds. What probably comes to their mind is the Catalonian equivalent of the Super Tuscan movement — concentrated reds made with international grapes by a band of outsiders in the '90s.

In Priorat there had long been scepticism towards native grapes. Garnacha wasn't seen as capable of making fine wines because of its high alcohol and tendency to rusticity, while Cariñena could often be too dilute. So when, in the late '80s, hippie and former *négociant* René Barbier arrived with his band of aspiring *vignerons*, they wasted no time planting noble French varieties. Barbier founded Clos Mogador, a communal winery with several projects under the one roof. Alongside him were Álvaro Palacios, who wanted to start a project away from his family estate in Rioja; Daphne Glorian of Clos Erasmus, who joined after meeting them by chance in an Orlando bar; José Luis Pérez of Clos Martinet and Carles Pastrana of Clos de L'Obac. Each project had 'Clos' in its name to emphasise their specific terroirs.

"Arriving in Priorat in '88 was like arriving on the moon," says Daphne Glorian, at home in the village of Gratallops. "I remember driving around one of the turns in the roads and being confronted by a sheer wall of rock. I thought to myself: This is something else!" Glorian made her debut Clos Erasmus with everyone "sorting grapes with one hand, and mixing cement with the other". But while Barbier's vision of putting Priorat on the then-Bordeaux-centric wine map was commendable, the lack of outside interest was worrying. "We had nothing and the banks wanted to repossess. Everyone was infighting," remembers José Luis Pérez's daughter Sara, who now runs Clos Martinet.

Everything changed in 1994 when the critic Robert Parker gave Clos Mogador a glowing review, and Priorat's rebirth as Spain's new fine-wine frontier began. It is the only Spanish region besides Rioja to hold the prestigious DOCa (Denominación de Origen Calificada) classification. "Parker's involvement made us jump ten years into the future," says Glorian. "No one was interested before then — especially in Spain." Calling her 1994 Clos Erasmus "one of the most exciting young wines anyone could possibly taste" and "a hypothetical blend of Pétrus, l'Évangile, Rayas Châteauneuf-du-Pape, and Napa's 1993 Colgin Cabernet Sauvignon", the Parker hype launched into overdrive.

Today Glorian has dropped most of the international grapes, making quality reds such as 2019 Clos Erasmus — at 15.5% ABV a punchy wine with

a backbone of slate-minerality. But I struggle with many wines of the '90s and '00s. Some, like the rated 2001 Clos Mogador, are tannic bodybuilders lacking generosity or finesse. Others, like 2006 Clos Martinet, a blend of Garnacha, Syrah and other grapes, are reminiscent of hot-vintage Gigondas. Much better are Sara Pérez's 2020 and 2021 Clos Martinets — which, although retaining a savoury Rhône twang, have lovely balance — as well as her finessed 'Els Escurçons', a light red in a fresher style.

Finesse is also the aim of Álvaro Palacios, whose single vineyard 'L'Ermita' *cuvée* emerged with Peter Sisseck's 'Pingus' as the most cult Spanish wines of the '90s. Palacios has an uncompromising work ethic, farming 40ha of Priorat hillsides. He started out clearing Clos Dofi's lost terraces, but his major coup came when he bought 'L'Ermita', a cool north-east-facing, high-altitude amphitheatre of 100-year-old-plus vines on the region's famous llicorella schist with quartz and sandy soils. A majestic Grand Cru in all but name, 2021 'L'Ermita' has an ethereal orange pith and raspberry fragrance with a dense but featherweight texture and a finish that I never wanted to end.

The veteran *vigneron* August Vicent of Gratallops' Celler Cecilio remembers Palacios as having "more sensitivity to listen to the old local people, rather than the others who wanted to re-invent Priorat". 'L'Ermita' is a wonderful example of building on such sensibilities, made from mostly Garnacha grown in costers planted directly into the slope's contours, a traditional method many producers are starting to use again. While terraces offer stability, costers enable higher planting densities, producing smaller berries with riper stems that some include in fermentations to retain a sense of freshness. Ripening fruit in Priorat is never a problem, but preserving acidity is.

Ester Nin and Carles Ortiz of Família Nin-Ortiz leave me in no doubt that the key to making a beautiful wine is all in the timing. Harvest too late and your wines are as refreshing as marmalade — too early and they'll have green flavours. When I visit them at their Porrera winery they are busy sorting grapes with their team and wearing T-shirts with 'pH 3.2' — their target acidity — printed in huge fonts on their backs. A crate of discarded raisins sits by the door. Their signature 'Planetes de Nin' is a transparent blend of Garnacha Tinta, Cariñena and the fabulously monikered Garnacha Peluda ('Hairy Garnacha'), with stone and raspberry aromas and silky tannins. It epitomises the purity that *vignerons* can achieve by abandoning blends of international grapes, as do Dominik Huber's Terroir al Límit wines.

Huber, originally from near Frankfurt, became intrigued with Catalonia after reading an article in *El País*. After getting experience with Clos Martinet, he set up Dits del Terra in 2001 with South African winemaker Eben Sadie, and three years later launched his own Terroir al Límit project. "The name Terroir al Límit is about being at the limit of being able to do something — being able to survive," says Huber of his early days in Priorat without a phone signal, internet coverage, or many other present-day essentials. Not to mention his ground-breaking wines being rejected by the appellation board for "lacking typicity", or the occasions that other *vignerons* ridiculed him for starting harvesting before them, or employing workers to sort through his grapes.

Huber uses whole-cluster fermentations of biodynamic fruit, likening winemaking to brewing tea using the highest-quality water at the ideal temperature and letting flavours gently infuse. Indeed, if I had to pick one wine as the antidote to outdated views of Priorat it would be 2019 Terroir al Límit 'Les Manyes'. Pure Garnacha Peluda from clay soils high in the mountains behind Scala Dei, 'Les Manyes' perfume of decaying strawberries, rose and dirt is reminiscent of some from the sainted crus of central eastern France. Another region based around a monastery where ancient soils and native grapes conjure thrilling wines? Some things seem almost mystically meant to be. ●

Terroir al Límit
'Les Manyes'
$$$$

Cellers de Scala Dei
'Masdeu de Scala Dei'
$$$

Família Nin-Ortiz
Nit de Nin 'Coma d'en Romeu'
$$$

Mas Martinet
'Els Escurçons'
$$$

Álvaro Palacios
'L'Ermita'
$$$$

2020 Mas Martinet 'Els Escurçons'.

MOUNTAIN SIZE
JOYFUL JUICE FROM OTHER SPANISH SLOPES

Envínate
Táganan 'Parcela Margalagua'
Tenerife
$$$

Guímaro
Ribeira Sacra
Galicia
$$–$$$

It's been amazing to witness Spain transform itself from dusty old has-been to the Most Exciting Wine Country in the World™ over the past decade. From Ribeira Sacra to the Gredos Mountains and Jerez, vignerons with a DIY attitude have been busy reviving abandoned vineyards full of native varieties, replacing the over-extracted, over-oaked styles of yore with freshness and finesse. Envínate Táganan 'Parcela Margalagua' encapsulates this theme: a sensual, rose and white pepper-perfumed red field blend of different grape varieties from ungrafted old vines high on Tenerife's mountainous north-east coast. (If ten years ago anyone had predicted vinous greatness from an island whose claim to fame was hosting rowdy squads of British holidaymakers who end every sentence with "yeah", they would have been considered a berry short of a bunch.) A collective of four winemakers piecing together guerrilla-style vineyard purchases and collaborations in Almansa, Extremadura, Ribeira Sacra and Tenerife, Envínate has become one of the hottest names in wines by thinking creatively.

Pedro Rodríguez Pérez is the fourth generation of his family to farm grapes in Ribeira Sacra, a Galician sub-region whose vertiginous vineyards looks like The Land that Time Forgot. His grandparents ran one of the few government-certified mills, where they'd wear out the soles of their shoes from operating the waterwheels 24 hours a day. Down-to-earth and perennially smiling, Pedro has taken his Guímaro domaine from strength to strength since dropping out of law school, and is credited, along with sometime partner Raúl Perez and Algueira's Fernando González Riveiro, as being among the first winemakers to draw international attention to Ribeira Sacra. Guímaro's whole-bunch single-vineyard Mencía-based field blend 'Finca Pombeiras' is a powerful wine that has beautiful finesse, while his Ribeira Sacra Mencía from these incredibly challenging to farm vineyards is a steal. "When I left Ribeira Sacra for the first time I thought: What? People plant vines on flat land?" says Pedro.

30

GROW YOUR OWN

Searching for individuality in English wine

Breaky Bottom,
on the South
Downs in East
Sussex, is a
contender for
England's most
idyllic vineyard.

"Sometimes you have to play a long time to be able to play like yourself."
Miles Davis

In 2015 and 2020, *Noble Rot* magazine organised tastings pitting leading English sparkling wines anonymously against Champagnes. Surprisingly, or not, depending on where you stand, Hambledon, a wine from Hampshire, won the first event (followed by Sussex's Nyetimber and Champagne's Pol Roger), and in 2020 came runner-up to Larmandier-Bernier, one of the original 'Champagne Growers'. English fizz had undoubtedly arrived, but increasingly something niggled. Sure, we produce better sparkling wine than ever, but so many domaines still base themselves on the Grandes Marques model, with an emphasis on corporate branding and consistency over character. Were we missing the fact that it was the Champagne Growers who were making some of the best wines anywhere by farming living soils, lowering yields, using native yeasts and putting the onus on 'somewhereness'?

Unlike the Champagne Growers' revolution, whose proximity to each other enabled them to share ideas and reimagine their bubbles as every bit as terroir-expressive as those of the sainted Burgundy crus to their south, the broad church of English wine is so much more spread out. There are no tenth-generation Kentish *vignerons* at hand to pass down centuries of knowledge, and huge investments in land and wineries are being made by people who've amassed fortunes in unrelated industries with unrealistic expectations and little experience of wine. Sure, most English winemakers have solid technical skills, many having graduated from East Sussex's Plumpton College. But understanding the magic of wine by actually drinking great bottles is usually a prerequisite to making them.

Adrian Pike and
Issy, Westwell
Wines, Kent.

Tasting god-like genius certainly helps, if only to make the huge effort and expense of wine production seem worthwhile (especially so with sparkling's secondary fermentation and long *élevage*). But if you don't know how good wine can be, or don't care, it's certainly easier to cynically harvest high yields of under-ripe fruit and manipulate them in the winery later. If it was me, before producing a drop I'd seek out the top producers and try to learn from them first. Hambledon didn't miss a trick seeking help from Pol Roger to make its world-class NV fizz. But who are the English dreamers making uncompromising, unique wines, like Champagne's David Léclapart or Jérôme Prévost?

I headed to the Sussex South Downs to meet a maverick who—though many English producers can be considered 'growers' in the sense that they farm their own grapes—is one of our originals. Down a dirt track peppered with axle-grinding potholes for a mile, or perhaps two, past grazing sheep and a wall of shocking white chalk cleaved clean out of the hillside, I arrive at a cottage that's straight out of the pages of an Enid Blyton novel. This is Breaky Bottom: no, not a fart joke, but the home of *vigneron*-raconteur Peter Hall, who, while perennially puffing on a roll-up cigarette (see p. 68), regales me with tales of his idiosyncratic life. "Born on a mountaintop in Tennessee, killed him a bear when he was only three," he begins. "It's difficult—you're going to have to cut my stories short."

Hall bought Breaky Bottom in 1974 and planted vineyards a couple of years later, inspired by Nick Poulter's book *Wines from Your Vines*. Flooded five times since, he hasn't always found making a living in this bucolic valley near Lewes easy, and has subsidised his métier with a second job. Today, though, Peter produces distinctive sparkling wines from the Champenois' trilogy of Chardonnay, Pinot Noir and Pinot Meunier, as well as a 100% Seyval Blanc—an oft-maligned hybrid grape that, against the odds, he crafts into a precise, age-worthy fizz. Able to refine his technique over a long period, he's created wines better thought of as an extension of the man himself: generous of spirit, and entirely of themselves. Indeed, Breaky Bottom's linear 2010 Seyval Blanc 'Cuvée Koizumi Yakumo Brut' is quite unlike any sparkling wine I've ever drunk. Not only do I admire how youthful it feels at ten years of age, but also how Hall has elevated a grape many have written off.

Fifty-five miles to the east near Ashford in Kent, Adrian Pike is another English 'Grower' employing low-fi winemaking. Formerly working in music running indie record label Moshi Moshi, Pike caught the wine bug and retrained at Plumpton College before raising £2 million to buy Westwell Wines. Producing the excellent sparkling 'Pelegrim', he also grows 2.5ha of Ortega, reimagining another somewhat maligned grape as a distinctive orange wine by fermenting it on its skins with some ageing in amphoras. Alongside Charlie Herring, Davenport, Offbeat and Tillingham, Westwell is at the forefront of England's still winemaking scene.

Henry and Kaye Laithwaite of Harrow & Hope are another couple following their own path in Marlow, Buckinghamshire. After years in Australia making "monstrous" Parker-style reds, the Laithwaites moved home and bought a paddock suitable for planting vines from searching property websites, something Henry says "would never happen now". Indeed, some parts of the Chiltern Hills remind me of eastern France's Jura, with west-facing slopes and chalk, gravel and clay soils. Planting vineyards

in 2010, their wines are benefiting from increasingly intense fruit as the plants age. And by moving to organic farming, using only wild yeasts for barrel ferments, and studiously picking at full ripeness, their strategy is more grounded than many would-be English superbrands.

"We don't have the budgets for advertising campaigns, so we focus on farming," says Henry. "I don't want to talk about luxury, or special moments: I can't do that because it makes me cringe. The first 20 years is about finding your feet. We've got to keep learning." With a lack of fellow *vignerons* living nearby, and some others putting a bombastic spin on everything English wine, Henry says he misses engaging in authentic conversations about winemaking. There's huge potential here, but it takes time to master your own style. "There are easier ways to make money, although they're probably not as much fun," says Henry. "I see this as a 100-year multi-generational project—even though my daughter says she's going to flog it and buy a pony." ●

Westwell
'Pelegrim' NV
Kent
$$$

Breaky Bottom
Seyval Blanc 'Cuvée Koizumi
Yakumo Brut' Vintage
East Sussex
$$$

Hambledon
Classic Cuvée NV
Hampshire
$$$

Wiston
Blanc de Blancs Vintage
West Sussex
$$$

Harrow & Hope
Brut Rosé Vintage
Buckinghamshire
$$$

Langham Wine
Dorset
$$$

Twenty-something Tommy Grimshaw held, for a time at least, the distinction of being England's youngest head winemaker, a reflection of both his competence and his impressive Langham wines. If others are interested in replicating the big Champagne houses' standard NV blends, wine-loving Grimshaw takes his inspiration from great Côte des Blancs growers such as Anselme Selosse and Pascal Agrapart, applying a similar ethos to making 'fine wine with bubbles'. Langham's vineyards are on Dorset chalk soils and their fruit is fermented in used oak barrels for breadth and subtly oxidative characteristics. Expect to see interesting developments here in coming years.

Sugrue South Downs
Sussex
$$$

Dermot Sugrue has long taken a Champagne 'Grower'-type approach to producing English sparkling wine. A graduate of Plumpton College, he spent time working at Pomerol's L'Église-Clinet as well as stints as head winemaker at Nyetimber and Wiston Estate, where he earned a reputation as one of the country's top vignerons. Having left Wiston (with, as I tasted, stocks of brilliant cuvées ageing on lees in their cellars for future release) he now focuses on his own project — Sugrue South Downs — with his winemaker wife Ana and boutique hotelier Robin Hutson.

Tim Phillips, Charlie Herring,
Hampshire.

Charlie Herring
Hampshire
$$$

Charlie Herring is actually a chap
called Tim Phillips, the owner of
one-acre of vines planted within a
once-abandoned 19th-century walled
kitchen garden located a couple of
miles from the Solent. Phillips
tends his idyllic, but undoubtedly
uncommercial, Hampshire vineyard
like a passionate amateur gardener
with very low costs. Having planted
Chardonnay, Riesling, Pinot Noir and
Sauvignon Blanc — not necessarily easy
grapes to grow in the English climate
— he also makes his wines without any
sulphur additions. In line with his
DIY approach, Phillips only sells
his tiny production of circa 2,500
bottles through an annual open day at
his rustic winery in a former barn,
supplementing his limited income from
winemaking with a few weeks of finance
work a year. It's what Phillips
describes as 'peasant economics'
at its best.

31

THE WILD CRUNCH

The Sciaccarellu renaissance, Corsica, France

The view from
Clos Canarelli
winery, Figari,
Corsica, France.

If you take one thing away from this book, aside from strategies for finding characterful vino or an impression of what it's like drinking the world's most fabled wine, let it be a curiosity for Sciaccarellu. No, not the hookah lounge on Edgware Road — although I hear it does a mean hubbly-bubbly. I'm talking about the red Corsican grape also known as Sciaccarello, Sciucitaghjolu or, in nearby Italy, Mammolo. It all depends on who you're talking to, and where their allegiances lie. Because the Corsicans are not an easy bunch to pin down. Corsica may officially be part of France, but most of its citizens have a disdain for La République that would've made coalition armies defeating Napoleon at Waterloo proud. Napoleon, coincidentally, is Corsica's most famous son — not that they'd tell you. Because, well… he's also French.

Pronounced "check-ar-ellu", Sciaccarellu — like Corsica's mineral white Vermentinu — will always have a place in my cellar. If I was restricted to describing it in two words, I might settle on 'Mediterranean elegance' — if that didn't sound like an aftershave ad. But, as a red Burgundy lover who revels in similarities with the sensual fragrance, fresh acidity and moderate tannins of that region, I'll defer to the late, great Puligny *vigneronne* Anne-Claude Leflaive, who compared it to "wild Pinot Noir" growing among the island's maquis shrubland. The Corsicans themselves say they love its 'crunch', Sciucitaghjolu meaning 'bursting or crunching under the tooth' in the local dialect.

But I'm not the only one who has developed a taste for Sciaccarellu. Even the Corsicans who've grown this pale, thin-skinned grape for decades seem to have recently undergone a collective awakening to its potential.

For when made as a pure single-variety *cuvée* – *'in purezza'*, as they say in neighbouring Tuscany – it can inspire levels of adoration that evade Corsican blends. Such an epiphany happened to Yves Canarelli, Figari AOC's top winemaker, when witnessing reactions to Sciaccarellu at a Hong Kong tasting. Convinced that "Sciaccarellu is the future", he returned home and made *in purezza* 'Alta Rocca', the 2019 vintage of which has a beautifully pure, raspberry-liqueur-like core. "The danger could be that all growers change to Sciaccarellu," says Canarelli, a supporter, like all the Corsicans I meet, of their treasure trove of indigenous grapes.

Sciaccarellu's heartlands are in the south of Corsica, where centuries ago the grape arrived from Tuscany as Mammolo. According to Jancis Robinson and co's encyclopedic *Wine Grapes*, *Viola mammolo* is the Italian name for *Viola odorata*, or sweet violet, referring to its perfume. Sciaccarellu is the main variety in Corsican red and rosé wine production, except in Patrimonio in the far north – the island's first-ever appellation – where allegiance is to another grape with Italian roots, Niellucciu, a.k.a. good old Sangiovese. Corsica's annual wine production is 68% rosé, 20% red and 12% white, but rosé is declining as wineries meet the rising international demand for white. But having tasted deftly handled Sciaccarellu – lightly extracted with no excessive oak – I know where I'd focus my energies.

South of the capital of Ajaccio, a roller-coaster car ride along hairpin roads (the Romans settled here, but even they couldn't build a straight road on such mountainous terrain), you'll find the pioneering Domaine Comte Abbatucci. Owned by Jean-Charles Abbatucci (descendant of another Jean-Charles Abbatucci, a highly decorated general in Napoleon's army for whom roads in Ajaccio are named), the domaine was founded in 1950 by his father Antoine, a determined campaigner who helped to preserve native grape varieties when many were being replanted with 'international' ones. Besides his biodynamic certification, Jean-Charles is known for sometimes using leftfield farming techniques such as playing traditional polyphonic music to his vines over loudspeakers and treating a soon-to-be released Sciaccarellu *cuvée* with sea water. Eccentric, maybe – but given how good that new wine tastes, it's clearly working.

Abbatucci's more conventional pure Sciaccarellu 'Monte Bianco' is a bold, smoky red wine that rounds out and opens up with exposure to oxygen. Its inherent southern richness reminds me a little of Brunello di Montalcino – but as with comparisons to Pinot Noir, generalising about grape varieties doesn't take into account the significant variables of winemaking philosophy and land. Nevertheless, today it's easy to join the dots between a movement of *vignerons* producing Pinot Noir, Nebbiolo, Nerello Mascalese, Grenache and now Sciaccarellu: wines that emphasise delicacy and freshness over robustness.

For years many people making 'fine' wine equated quality with uber-concentrated colour and material, and extended ageing in new oak. But these techniques are out of step with modern tastes: especially so with Sciaccarellu, which loses clarity when overworked, developing bacon-like aromas. "We don't do an extraction – it's an infusion," says 28-year-old Guillaume Seroin of Domaine Sant 'Armettu in the southern appellation of Sartène. Its flagship 'Myrtus' – a blend of Sciaccarellu, Grenache et al. – sure isn't bad, but it doesn't transport me the way the

vivid scent of ripe strawberries and maquis shrubland does in its pure Sciaccarellu 'Rosumarinu'. Better still is top pure *cuvée* 'L'Ermite', which pops with colour like the bougainvillea flowers that blaze around the estate.

Sciaccarellu was rarely made as a single-variety *cuvée* until pioneering domaines such as Abbatucci and Clos Capitoro came along; now it is among France's great terroir-specific wines. And none more so than those of Gérard Courrèges of Domaine de Vaccelli in Ajaccio AOC, who made his name with 'Granit' — a single-vineyard Sciaccarellu with a minimalist label that's become a brand in itself. Courrèges dreamed of becoming a restaurateur until he was served Sciaccarellu alongside roasted lamb with figs and honey by friends of his parents as a teenager — a Sciaccarellu road-to-Damascus moment. Courrèges has a passion for Côte de Nuits classics and discussing wine with him is like talking to a Burgundian — albeit substituting Sciaccarellu and Vermentinu for Pinot Noir and Chardonnay. Aside from his elegant, pale-coloured standard 'Granit', he also makes 'Granit 60' — a Sciaccarellu aged in concrete eggs, sold only to customers on Corsica — and 'Granit 174', a smoky, silken, herb-inflected beauty from a tiny 0.174ha site.

Like most of Corsica, Courrèges's hillside vineyards are made of granite. But there are pockets of limestone and red clay in Patrimonio, on which one of the appellation's leading winemakers, Muriel Giudicelli, has planted Sciaccarellu. Already making world-class Vermentinu — "a love story: it's easy to make" — and Nielucciu — "harder to ripen with a rusticity that demands time in bottle to soften" — she's unsurprisingly succumbed to the charms of Corsica's wild Pinot Noir, and wants to prove it can be just as successfully grown in the north. Sciaccarellu, it seems, is irrepressible — let's just hope it doesn't become a victim of its own success. ●

Gérard Courrèges, Domaine de Vaccelli, Ajaccio, Corsica.

Domaine de Vaccelli
'Granit' Rouge
Ajaccio
$$$

Clos Canarelli
'Alta Rocca'
Figari
$$$

Domaine Comte Abbatucci
'Monte Bianco'
Ajaccio
$$$

Sant'Armettu
'Rosumarinu'
Sartène
$$

Sant'Armettu
'L'Ermite'
Sartène
$$$

32

YOU DON'T HAVE TO BE RICH TO CELLAR GREAT WINE

Investing in the Bank of Future Vinous Joys

Sommelier Ali
Duncan with
vigneron Benoît
Moreau in the
cellars of Noble
Rot, Lamb's
Conduit Street,
London.

Through good times and bad, thick or thin, building your own wine cellar can be a constant source of pleasure. Okay, maybe not an actual bricks-and-mortar cellar, with real-life creepy-crawlies and mould covering the walls. But a handful of choice bottles bought from an independent wine shop, stored in an understairs cupboard or a Eurocave refrigeration unit, will only mean more joy.

There are many reasons why people start cellaring wine. The forward-thinking 'bon viveur' recognises that quality wines gain complexity with age, taking pleasure investing in their future happiness. The switched-on 'aficionado' knows their Julien Labet from their Lafon-Rochet, squirrel-ling away bottles from exciting new *vignerons* before social media catches on and prices rise. And, of course, all kinds of collecting involving serious moolah attracts the 'borderline sex offender OCD weirdo' who, with civilisation teetering on the brink of an apocalypse that'll make Bosch's 'The Last Judgment' look like Club Tropicana, stockpiles acclaimed crus so they can drink a glass of something 'profound' when everything goes south. As fans of *The Fabulous Furry Freak Brothers* know: "Dope will get you through times of no money better than money will get you through times of no dope." Ditto Chambertin-Clos de Bèze and Armageddon.

But starting a stellar cellar needn't mean focusing on expensive Bur-gundy (although if you can get access to domaines at 50% or less of market value on release from the importer, and are able to drink half and sell the other half to cover your outlay, fill your boots). Because, just as anyone who hasn't been living under a rock, or in Croydon, for the past decade will tell you, now is the best time in history to be a wine lover. Frankly, why get upset that you'll never drink 1947 Cheval Blanc when there's an ever-expanding galaxy of very affordable, authentic, flavourful wines that can form the foundation of a cellar that'll see you right for many years?

If you've only ever bought wine by the bottle as and when you need, but fancy starting a small collection, I recommend spending an initial £750 on 12 bottles at circa £62 each. That could be six bottles each of two wines, or four different three-bottle cases — which, as you watch them change over time, will help you form a real opinion. There's no guarantee that any wine will improve with age, but the best guide is the producer, and whether or not they have the faintest idea about what they are doing. This should mean they farm high-quality vineyards without fertilisers and pesticides, harvest low yields of ripe, intense fruit, and refrain from fucking around with the grape like some kind of wannabe Dr Frankenstein. Low yields help get good concentration of extract and polyphenols, thus 'structure' — the mix of acidity, tannin and natural preservatives that gives wine longevity.

So, what bottles should you look for, and where should you buy them? Well, given most supermarket wine is to authenticity what Pot Noodle is to Szechuan cuisine, Morrisons is not the place to earmark cases for your firstborn's wedding. But that doesn't mean cheaper wine should be uninteresting, or full of Novichok-grade 'preservatives', and purchasing respected domaines as close to source as possible — i.e. by the case from the importer — is the best way to do it. Opposite are some trustworthy merchants and strategies to help you get going. ●

HOW TO BUY GREAT BOTTLES
RELIABLE WINE-FINDING TOOLS AND TRADERS

Wine-Searcher.com and
CellarTracker.com
Essential websites

Farr Vintners
Battersea, London

When in 1999 www.wine-searcher.com launched, it single-handedly made buying fine wine easier than ever, while vastly reducing the odds of finding a stash of bargain Hermitage in an obscure wine shop ever again. Billed as the 'Google of wine', the website collects online wine lists from retailers and auction houses around the world every day, making finding that rare bottle, or most competitively priced case, a doddle. It's worth paying for Wine-Searcher's premium PRO subscription to access its comprehensive listings. But be careful from whom you buy — especially brokers who don't actually hold the stock they advertise. Another popular website, CellarTracker.com, can be a useful tool, featuring a huge database of user reviews. Rather than professional critics' snapshots of infant wines, aggregated amateur reviews of bottles that have actually been drunk can provide useful insights, such as highlighting cuvées that suffer especially high incidences of cork taint, premature oxidation and other faults.

Trusting who you buy wine from is vital, and one of the most not just trustworthy, but knowledgeable, merchants I know is Farr Vintners' Stephen Browett. Browett joined Farr Vintners — which was founded in 1978 in an 11th-floor Acton council flat — in 1984 having worked his way up from being a delivery-van driver to buying assistant at a Knightsbridge merchant. Decades later he bought the whole company, transforming it into one of the world's leading traders selling huge quantities of fine wine. Browett is a go-getter with a deep knowledge of Cru Classé Claret and a penchant for blind tasting, loving nothing more than promoting inexpensive wines that outperform similar ones at many times the price. Whereas in the past many modern traders weren't knowledgeable about the fine wine they were selling, and erudite old-school merchants lacked business savvy, Farr Vintners' ability to marry the two is what makes them an excellent company to buy wine from. As does their fearlessness in giving customers a reality check on what really makes it worth buying.

(Other reliable merchants and importers you should try include Blast Vintners, Turville Valley, Hatton & Edwards, Hedonism, Seckford Wines, Berry Bros & Rudd, Barber Wines, Vine Trail, Yapp Brothers, Raeburn Fine Wines and Les Caves de Pyrene.)

Shrine to the Vine
Lamb's Conduit Street and
Broadway Market, London

I'm not impartial, but it'd be remiss
not to mention that Shrine to the
Vine is here to supply the vino of
your dreams. Part of Keeling Andrew
imports — which my business partner
Mark Andrew and I founded in 2017 —
the shops and website are our attempt
to recreate the kind of places we love
to buy bottles ourselves, ranging from
exciting natural wines to venerable
vintages of classic domaines. Mark and
I met at Roberson Wine, a shop on a
moribund stretch of Kensington High
Street where we both worked (Mark in
the shop, me as MD of Island Records
next door), and became drinking
buddies, egging each other on to
explore the outer reaches of wine. I
remember how exciting it was to visit
Roberson, not knowing what I would
find on the shelves. That feeling
still resonates with us today — a
thirst for discovering what lies under
the next cork.

1728	Vino Pancho Romano, Jerez-Xérès-Sherry
1862	T.T.C. Lomelino Verdelho, Madeira
1928	Château d'Yquem, Sauternes
1934	R López de Heredia, Viña Tondonia Tinto, Rioja
1937	Domaine de la Romanée-Conti, Romanée-Conti
1945	Château Léoville-Poyferré, St-Julien
1945	Château Mouton Rothschild, Pauillac
1950	Château Cheval Blanc, St-Émilion
1959	Château Mouton Rothschild, Pauillac
1961	Château Latour, Pauillac
1964	R López de Heredia, Viña Tondonia Blanco, Rioja
1971	Salon, Champagne 'Le Mesnil'
1975	Château Lafleur, Pomerol
1978	Domaine de Montille, Volnay Premier Cru 'Les Taillepieds'
1978	Domaine Dujac, Gevrey-Chambertin Premier Cru 'Aux Combottes'
1978	Simon Bize, Savigny-lès-Beaune Premier Cru 'Aux Vergelesses'
1978	Domaine Jacques Puffeney, Arbois Vin Jaune
1982	Domaine de Trévallon, Coteaux des Baux en Provence
1983	Domaine Chave, Hermitage Rouge
1983	Domaine Leflaive, Puligny-Montrachet Premier Cru 'Les Pucelles'
1983	Domaine Ponsot, Morey-St-Denis Premier Cru 'Monts-Luisants' Blanc
1985	Domaine Ponsot, Clos de la Roche 'Cuvée Vieilles Vignes'
1986	Domaine Chave, Hermitage Blanc
1988	Château Rayas, Châteauneuf-du-Pape
1988	Domaine Jasmin, Côte-Rôtie
1989	Château Haut-Brion, Pessac-Léognan
1989	Domaine Raveneau, Chablis Grand Cru 'Valmur'
1990	Denis Bachelet, Charmes-Chambertin
1990	Domaine Charles Joguet, Chinon 'Clos de la Dioterie'
1990	Valentini, Trebbiano d'Abruzzo
1990	Il Paradiso di Manfredi, Brunello di Montalcino
1991	Domaine Jean-Louis Grippat, St-Joseph
1992	Domaine Trimbach, Riesling 'Clos Ste Hune'
1993	Domaine Michel Lafarge, Volnay Premier Cru 'Clos des Chênes'
1995	Domaine Chave, Ermitage 'Cuvée Cathelin'
1995	Domaine Gramenon, Côtes du Rhône 'A Pascal S'
1996	Domaine Coche-Dury, Meursault 'Les Rougeots'
1996	Domaine Roulot, Meursault Premier Cru 'Les Perrières'
1998	Domaine Grange des Pères, Vin de Pays de l'Hérault Rouge
1998	Château Haut-Brion, Pessac-Léognan
1998	Domaine Noël Verset, Cornas
1999	Domaine Leflaive, Chevalier-Montrachet
2000	Domaine Jacques-Frédéric Mugnier, Musigny
2002	Domaine du Comte Liger-Belair, La Romanée
2002	Verget, St Véran Terres Noires 'Atom Heart Mother'

2002	Emmanuel Houillon-Pierre Overnoy, Arbois Pupillin Ploussard
2002	Château Latour, Pauillac
2002	Krug, Champagne 'Clos du Mesnil'
2004	Soldera, Brunello di Montalcino Riserva
2004	Domaine Economou, 'Antigone', Crete
2005	Domaine de la Romanée-Conti, Romanée-Conti
2006	Bartolo Mascarello, Barolo
2006	Giuseppe Rinaldi, Barolo 'Brunate'
2006	Paolo Bea, Montefalco Sagrantino 'Pagliaro'
2006	Domaine de la Romanée-Conti, Richebourg
2006	François Rousset-Martin, Château-Chalon 'Voile No. 6'
2007	Weingut Keller, Riesling Grosses Gewächs 'Kirchspiel'
2007	Domaine Vincent Dauvissat, Chablis Grand Cru 'Les Preuses'
2007	Domaine Armand Rousseau, Chambertin
2007	Montevertine, Toscana 'Le Pergole Torte'
2008	Domaine Jacques-Frédéric Mugnier, Chambolle-Musigny Premier Cru 'Les Amoureuses'
2008	Stella di Campalto, Brunello di Montalcino
2008	Jérôme Prévost, Champagne La Closerie, 'Les Béguines'
2009	Domaine Roulot, Meursault Premier Cru 'Les Perrières'
2010	Hubert Lamy, St-Aubin Premier Cru 'Derrière Chez Edouard Haute Densité'
2010	Domaine Auguste Clape, Cornas
2010	Clos Rougeard, Saumur-Champigny 'Le Bourg'
2010	Gravner, Ribolla, Venezia Giulia
2014	Château-Grillet
2016	Domaine Cécile Tremblay, Chapelle-Chambertin
2016	Domaine Georges Mugneret-Gibourg, Échézeaux
2016	Richard Leroy, Vin de France 'Les Noëls de Montbenault'
2017	Domaine Lamy-Caillat, Chassagne-Montrachet Premier Cru 'La Romanée'
2017	Tenuta di Carleone, Toscana 'Uno'
2018	Domaine Pierre Gonon, St-Joseph
2018	Comando G, Sierra de Gredos 'Camino del Pilar'
2018	Les Vignes de Paradis, Vin des Allobroges 'Sous Voile'
2018	Domaine Georges Vernay, Condrieu 'Coteau de Vernon'
2019	Domaine de Vaccelli, 'Granit 174', Ajaccio
2019	Domaine Belluard, 'Le Feu', Savoie
2019	Stéphane Bernaudeau, 'Les Nourrissons', Loire
2019	Domaine Arnoux-Lachaux, Romanée-St-Vivant
2020	Guffens-Heynen, Pouilly-Fuissé 'Croux et Petits-Croux'
2020	Benoît Moreau, Bâtard-Montrachet
2021	Álvaro Palacios, 'L'Ermita', Priorat
2022	Suertes del Marqués, Listán Blanco 'Edición 1', Tenerife
NV	Champagne Jacques Selosse, 'Substance'
NV	Equipo Navazos, 'La Bota de Oloroso 94' Jerez-Xérès-Sherry

GLOSSARY

Appellation
In France an AOC (Appellation d'Origine Contrôlée) or AOP (Appellation d'Origine Protégée) is the district where a wine is certified to have come from. See also DO, DOCa, DOCG, VDP and PDO.

Barrique
A relatively small wooden barrel used for fermenting and/or ageing wine, the most commonly used of which are the Bordeaux *barrique* (which holds 225 litres) and the Burgundy *barrique* (228 litres).

Biodynamic viticulture
A form of farming and vineyard management based on the teachings of Rudolf Steiner.

Blanc de Blancs
Champagne made exclusively from white grapes, typically Chardonnay.

Blanc de Noirs
Champagne made exclusively from black grapes, typically Pinot Noir and Pinot Meunier.

Botte/Botti
Large Italian wood cask(s) for fermenting and/or ageing wine. Typically made of Slavonian oak.

Botrytis See **Noble rot**.

Grower Champagnes
Champagnes made by the owners of the estate where the grapes are grown. This is part of a growing movement to highlight wines that reflect their place of origin. RM on the label, meaning *récoltant-manipulant*, indicates that the contents are not made using bought-in grapes from various anonymous vineyards.

Brettanomyces
The yeast Brettanomyces bruxellensis, also known as 'brett', is a wine fault. The chemical compounds it produces smell like medical plasters, sweaty leather saddles and barnyards. While many drinkers hate it, others feel it adds complexity at low levels.

Climat
French, especially Burgundian, term for a specific vineyard site.

Cru
French word for a vineyard, or 'growth'. A 'Cru Classé' is one that has been classified. 'Premier Cru' (First Growth) and 'Grand Cru' (Great Growth) have specific meanings, depending on the region where they are used.

Cuvée
A specific batch of wine.

DO, DOCa
Denominación de Origen (DO) is the Spanish equivalent of AOC. Denominación de Origen Calificada (DOCa) is a higher level, currently conferred only in Rioja and Priorat.

DOCG
Denominazione di Origine Controllata e Garantita is the Italian equivalent of AOC, on which it was modelled.

Dosage
A sugary final addition to sparkling wine that determines sweetness.

Élevage
The process of ageing, or 'raising', a wine between fermentation and bottling.

Field blend
A mixture of different grape varieties planted within the same vineyard.

Flor See **Sous voile**.

First Growths
The top classified châteaux in Bordeaux: Haut-Brion, Lafite, Latour, Margaux, Mouton Rothschild and d'Yquem. See also **Cru**.

Grande Marque
Large producer, typically a *négociant*, in Champagne. Translates as 'big brand'.

Grosses Gewächs
Superior category for German dry wines launched by VDP in 2002.

IGT
Indicazione Geografica Tipica, or indication of geographical typicality, is one of four recognised classifications in Italian wine legislation.

Kabinett/Spätlese/Auslese
Three common Prädikat categories of German Rieslings relating to grape ripeness at harvest.

Lieu-dit
The given name of a specific plot of land within a larger appellation (although not an appellation itself).

Monopole
French term for a vineyard that belongs to a single owner.

Négociant
A producer who buys grapes or wine from third parties to sell under their own label.

Noble rot
A.k.a. Botrytis cinerea, a fungus that, given the right conditions, shrivels ripe white grapes on the vine, concentrating their sugars and making them ideal for producing the world's finest sweet wines.

NV
Non-vintage wine made by blending the production of different years.

Ouillé
French term for a wine that has been regularly topped up while ageing in barrel to produce a fresh, orthodox style. Used in the Jura to differentiate *ouillé* from non-topped-up, 'sous-voile' and oxidative styles.

Own-rooted vine
A vine that has not been grafted on to an American rootstock to protect against phylloxera.

PDO
Protected Designation of Origin is a term used in wine-making countries such as England, Wales and Greece to indicate that all aspects of production, processing and preparation of the grapes take place within the designated region.

GLOSSARY

Phylloxera
The aphid that attacks the roots of vines and gained notoriety by devastating vast swathes of European vineyards in the late 19th century.

Premature oxidation
A.k.a. premox is a problem famously affecting white Burgundies, among other wines, where seemingly random bottles oxidise at an unusually rapid rate and become out of condition long before their time.

Sélection massale
A.k.a. massal selection is a traditional technique used for replanting vineyards with cuttings of many exceptional old vines. It promotes diversity of plant material in the vineyard, as opposed to clonal selection, which uses the genetics of a single mother vine.

Solera
A system of barrel-ageing and fractional blending commonly used for consistency in Sherry.

Sous voile
Term used in Jura for wines made 'under a veil' of yeast cells, producing a style reminiscent of some Sherries (where the veil is called *flor*).

Terroir
French definition of a vineyard's total natural environment (including the hand of the winemaker). Wines of 'terroir' have a unique sense of 'somewhereness'.

Traditional method
A technique to produce high-quality sparkling wine through a secondary fermentation inside bottle. Previously known as the *Méthode Champenoise*.

VDP
In France, until 2009, VDP used to denote Vin de Pays but it has since been superseded by IGP (Indication Géographique Protégée). In terms of hierarchy, the IGP category is above Vin de France and below Appellation d'Origine Controllée (AOC). Separately, in Germany, VDP refers to Verband Deutscher Prädikatsweingüter, an organisation that designates the country's top-quality wines and estates.

Vigneron(ne)
Grower-winemaker with weathered hands and dirt under their nails.

Village wine
Burgundian term for a wine made from grapes grown in vineyards assigned a village-level appellation, e.g. Vosne-Romanée.

Vintage
Can mean either the year in which a wine was made, or the physical process of the harvest.

Volatile acidity
A wine fault at high levels, when it can smell like nail-polish remover and/or vinegar. In smaller doses it can add complexity and lift.

ACKNOWLEDGEMENTS

Jeroboams of thanks to everyone who has helped make *Who's Afraid of Romanée-Conti?* such fun to write. Sarah Lavelle and all at Quadrille Publishing, sub-editors Nick Funnell, Frankie McCoy, Stephanie Evans and Kate Hawkings, Matt Willey, Jonny Sikov and August Dine at Pentagram Design, photographers Benjamin McMahon, Tom Cockram and Juan Trujillo Andrades, Tim Bates at Peters Fraser & Dunlop, Marina O'Loughlin, Kermit Lynch, Perrine Fenal, Aubert de Villaine, Bertrand de Villaine, William Kelley, Charlie Lewis, Ollie McSwiney, Terri Seeber, Joshua Castle and all at Rotter Towers, Lauren Fonda, Robert Weiss, Jacq Burns, Diana Henry, Remus Brett, Jancis Robinson, Alexander Gilmour and Harriet Fitch Little at *The FT Weekend*, Stephen Browett, Quim Villa, Pepe Raventós, Frédéric Engerer, Mark Hedges, Mick Dean, John Hegarty, Alex Bond, Andrew Lewis, Vérane Frédiani, Franck Ribière, and my amazing mother Lorna Keeling. *Who's Afraid of Romanée-Conti?* would not have been possible without the friendship, tenacity and joie de vivre of my pal and business partner Mark Andrew. And the love and support of my wife Naomi Keeling, all-round beautiful soul and arbiter of good taste.

This book is dedicated to wine lovers past, present and future.

Chin chin.

Managing Director and Editor
Sarah Lavelle

Art Direction
Dan Keeling

Design
Matt Willey and Jonny Sikov, Pentagram

Copy Editors
Nick Funnell and Frankie McCoy

Design Manager, Quadrille
Katherine Case

Head of Production
Stephen Lang

Production Controller
Gary Hayes

First published in 2024 by Quadrille,
an imprint of Hardie Grant Publishing.

Quadrille
52–54 Southwark Street
London SE1 1UN
quadrille.com

Text © Dan Keeling 2024

Cataloguing in Publication Data: a catalogue record for this book
is available from the British Library.

ISBN
9781787139886

Printed in China

The publisher has made every effort to contact copyright holders.
We apologise in advance for any unintentional omissions and
would be pleased to insert the appropriate acknowledgement in
any subsequent edition.

Note
Page 33 'What to Pour for People Who Couldn't Care Less',
page 39 'The Restaurateur's Holiest of Grails', page 61 'A Wine
Cellar State of Mind' and page 91 'Bad to the Beaune' first
appeared in the *Financial Times*.

ABOUT THE AUTHOR

Dan Keeling is a London-based writer, restaurateur and wine merchant. He is editor and co-founder of *Noble Rot* magazine, and co-owner of its three eponymous London restaurants, which have won 'Wine List of the Year' at both the World Restaurant Awards and the National Restaurant Awards (the latter an unprecedented five times). Keeling Andrew, the wine import company he co-owns, represents some of the world's most exciting winemakers and offers bottles to the public through its Shrine to the Vine retail wine shops. Dan's first book *Noble Rot: Wine from Another Galaxy* (co-written with Mark Andrew) was The Guild of Food Writers 'Drinks Book of the Year 2021', and he has been awarded one Fortnum & Mason and three Louis Roederer awards for his writing about wine and food. He is also a contributor to *FT Weekend Magazine*. Dan previously worked in music as MD of Island Records and Head of A&R at Parlophone Records, where he signed Coldplay, Lily Allen, Athlete, and Bombay Bicycle Club, among others.